MONTEZUMA
THE CASTLE IN THE WEST

JON BOWMAN, EDITOR

NEW MEXICO
MAGAZINE

COPYRIGHT 2002

◆ ◆ ◆ ◆ ◆ ◆

Publisher: Ethel Hess
Editor: Jon Bowman
Photo Editor: Bette Brodsky
Book Design & Production: Bette Brodsky
Copy Editors: Jon Bowman, Walter K. Lopez

Library of Congress
Catalog Card Number: 2001-135825
ISBN: 0-937206-72-5 (hardcover)
0-937206-73-3 (softcover)

FRONT COVER: Montezuma Hotel circa 1903
Courtesy of Museum of New Mexico, Neg. No. 14726

TITLE PAGE : Montezuma Hotel after recent renovation.
Las Vegas Hot Springs, NM
Photo: Polly Mullen

TABLE OF CONTENTS

4   PREFACE
Jon Bowman

8   INTRODUCTION
Queen Noor

10   BIRTH OF THE CASTLE
Philip O. Geier

20   THE RICH & FAMOUS
Jon Bowman

26   RESORT FIT FOR ROYALTY
Heidi Utz

32   THEN AND NOW
Nancy Hanks & Mark Thaler

40   RENOVATION PORTFOLIO
Polly Mullen, Chun Y Lai & Bette Brodsky

100   ONE WORLD UNITED
Craig Smith

106   MONTEZUMA MEMORIA
Elmo Baca

112   THE ENDANGERED LIST

118   NEW MEXICO HERITAGE
PRESERVATION ALLIANCE

122   ABOUT THE CONTRIBUTORS

124   SUGGESTED READINGS

126   INDEX

Montezuma Compound, circa 1885

Bath house and old Stone Hotel at left, train depot in foreground.

Courtesy Citizens Committee for Historic Preservation, Las Vegas, New Mexico,

Photograph No. 0833, CCHP # 3380-1

Tony Sanchez Collection

Montezuma: Sparkling Jewel of the Southwest

By Jon Bowman

With the assistance of United World College President Phil Geier and Bill Richardson, first senior fellow at the Bartos Institute for the Constructive Engagement of Conflict

Before its renovation, the Montezuma Castle always struck me as the unpolished gem in the crown of New Mexico. The building itself is one of the most impressive in the American Southwest. I have been captivated by it for as long as I can remember. Over the past 20 years, the Montezuma and its environs have been home to the American campus of a worldwide educational program known as the United World College movement.

Today, we celebrate the successful renovation of the Montezuma. But it was not always so certain that the historic building would have a fate other than that of a crumbling remnant of another era. Major structural damage, prohibitive expense and the immensity of the undertaking all argued against saving the Montezuma. So has the fact that the United World College's primary objective is international education, not historic preservation. And since the United World College strives to build a worldwide network of the most promising teen-agers, it faces the constant challenge of raising resources to support its mission and its students.

In 1981, Prince Charles invited Armand Hammer and his foundation to establish an American campus of the United World College movement, which now encompasses 10 campuses and more than 100 voluntary national committees. The Montezuma Castle was then on the market, having been a seminary for 30 years, and Hammer chose it to house the new school. This was not to be, however, as the extent of the work required to bring the Castle back to useful life was far beyond the resources then available. Instead, the new school took root in the buildings surrounding the Montezuma, leaving the Castle as only a picturesque backdrop rather than the centerpiece of the idealistic and global school.

More recently, the compelling vision and leadership of the United World College's President Phil Geier has led to saving and adaptively reusing the Montezuma Castle. An American historian and someone with a keen interest in the material arts, Phil Geier also has been captivated by the Montezuma. In the 1990s he spearheaded an effort to gain national recognition for the historic building. Assisted by Kak Slick, one of New Mexico's greatest advocates for historic preservation, Phil was very successful in attracting attention to the Montezuma.

In 1997, the Montezuma was selected by the National Trust for Historic Preservation as one of "America's 11 Most Endangered Historic Places." In 1998, the White House Millennium Council named the Montezuma as one of "America's Treasures," the first property west of the Mississippi River to be so honored. With the Montezuma's significance validated and promoted by these national awards, the

PREFACE

challenge of raising the necessary funds for the building's renovation seemed a bit less daunting. In 1998, philanthropist Shelby M.C. Davis announced a major challenge grant, attracting funds from numerous other sources, both within and outside New Mexico, to save the Montezuma Castle.

Saving an important historic landmark is reason enough to celebrate, particularly as it sets a fine example for emulation elsewhere in this country and throughout the world. But saving the Montezuma is exciting beyond the preservation of a glorious 19th-century structure that has meant so much to the history of New Mexico and the American West. Restoring a building is one thing. Using the building in an extraordinary way to serve the world in the 21st century is quite another.

The renovated Montezuma is today an exciting international center. Students come from around the world to live, eat, play and learn in it. Those who, in many ways and many places over the decades ahead, will be deciding matters of global significance will have developed their skills, attitudes and global relationships in the Montezuma Castle as United World College students.

Particularly meaningful is that the Montezuma Castle also houses a new and promising conflict resolution initiative being undertaken by the United World College. The Bartos Institute for the Constructive Engagement of Conflict exists to bring together the world's diverse approaches to conflict resolution. The Montezuma Castle is the venue for this interchange involving diverse practitioners of conflict engagement. Just as the United World College brings together a wide range of students of different ethnic, religious, racial and national backgrounds, so it will bring together a variety of the world's approaches to addressing conflict. Bill Richardson, former United Nations ambassador, has been named the first of a worldwide group of Senior Fellows to become associated with this new institute. He foresees the Montezuma Castle as an ideal venue for both international and domestic conflict resolution dialogues.

When the Atchison, Topeka & Santa Fe railway built the Montezuma in the 1880s, nearby Las Vegas was the commercial hub of the Southwest and the Montezuma was an exclusive way to experience the romance of the West. Today, we see the world with different eyes and from a changing vantage point. New Mexico is at the crossroads of the North-South NAFTA and the East-West/Atlantic-Pacific virtual highways. The new Montezuma is the inclusive way to experience the world.

The Montezuma Castle is a great structure, significant for its history, and all the more important for its renovation. But most important of all is its future promise to both New Mexico and the larger world. The Montezuma is now a polished gem in the crown of New Mexico.

Touring Carriages, Montezuma, circa 1886

Courtesy Citizens Committee for Historic Preservation, Las Vegas, New Mexico,

Photograph No. 1211, CCHP # 2024-5

ERB Collection, Methodist Church

Her Majesty Queen Noor of Jordan on September 29, 2001, the first public unveiling of the castle's renovation. Montezuma, NM.

Photo: Polly Mullen

Testimony to the Human Spirit
By Her Majesty Queen Noor of Jordan

Residents and visitors alike agree that New Mexico's natural beauty is truly breathtaking. More than aesthetic delight, however, experiencing New Mexico is also an awe-inspiring journey, imbued with a deep sense of spirituality. New Mexico's tripartite culture, combining Native American, Hispanic and Anglo-European influences, further accents its unique environment.

Tangible expressions of this multicultural diversity add to the landscape and remind us of history's unforeseen turn of events, their interplay with one another over time and their residual effect on our contemporary lives. New Mexico's various architectural styles and buildings provide insight into social, economic and cultural traits of the past and afford a wealth of opportunities not only for retaining and respecting those heritages but also for giving shape to a vibrant future as well.

This is certainly evident with the Montezuma, a Victorian castle in the New Mexican high desert, which has a lively history now spanning three centuries. Perhaps more than a compelling history of an important building, this volume is a testimony to the human spirit, especially in terms of innovation and perseverance. It gives perspective to the appeal of natural resources and how humanity exploits these precious gifts for our own objectives. The whole experience of renovating and saving the Castle validates the significance of historic preservation and, I believe, sets a fine example for others around the world to follow.

This book also documents the tremendous energy and strength of the United World College movement, as the Montezuma Castle is the centerpiece of our American campus. In saving the Castle, the United World College movement has found new and creative ways to bridge the past and the future, to bring innovative ideas and programs into being, and to demonstrate in another way how everything in this world is at once both local and global. The Castle's renovation into a multifaceted international center will also add significantly to New Mexico's already striking cultural landscape.

The chronicle of Montezuma Castle reminds us that life is indeed full of innumerable and unpredictable challenges and setbacks. More importantly, though, its successful completion affirms our vast human potential as we strive to realize our aspirations for a better world.

Her Majesty Queen Noor of the Hashemite Kingdom of Jordan has served as voluntary president of the United World Colleges since 1995.

INTRO-
DUCTION

Group on burros in front of Adobe Hotel

Las Vegas Hot Springs, NM

Photo by James N. Furlong

Courtesy of Museum of New Mexico, Neg. No. 13886916

Montezuma: Myth and Symbol of the American West

By Philip O. Geier, Ph.D.

Myths and symbols of the American West have long captured our imagination and no more so than at the time when the "frontier" was fully receding and disappearing. In 1890, the U.S. Census Bureau declared the frontier officially closed. At about the same time, historian Frederick Jackson Turner advanced his frontier hypothesis that was to alter and influence the study of American history for most of the next century. The West, Turner metaphorically described, is "a magic fountain of youth in which America continually bathed and was rejuvenated."

The allure of the West prompted one of the greatest voluntary mass migrations in history, with some half-million Americans uprooting from the East and taking trails, like the Santa Fe Trail, west between 1800 and 1870. After 1870, access to and settlement of the West was greatly accelerated by the arrival of the railroad. The Atchison, Topeka & Santa Fe Railway forever changed the face and complexion of New Mexico.

Construction of the Santa Fe railroad began in Topeka, Kansas, when the first shovelful of earth was turned over on October 30, 1868. By July 1879, it arrived in Las Vegas, then New Mexico's hub city. Las Vegas became the transportation and commercial center of the Southwest and maintained that status until early in the 20th century. This was a time of far-reaching cultural, social and economic changes as people of different backgrounds poured into New Mexico, altering the established Indian and Hispanic cultures, both largely agrarian and, at least nominally, Roman Catholic.

The newcomers, almost regardless of national origins, ethnicity or race, became known as "Anglos" since their common language was English. Along with the Anglos came technological innovations and new economic institutions that radically altered the pastoral character of such New Mexican places as Las Vegas, "the meadows." And, as we shall see with the birth of the Montezuma, the Anglo influence brought architectural styles never before seen in New Mexico.

The moving force behind these changes was the railroad, which became the most inventive promoter of the myths and symbols of the American West to Easterners and Europeans. The Santa Fe railroad, for example, glorified its own role in "civilizing the West" in its romantic publications circulated to patrons. The following segment, describing the railroad as transforming the desert into a garden, is taken from a Santa Fe publication of 1887:

BIRTH OF THE CASTLE

> It [the railroad] came creeping slowly across the face of the desert like an attenuated smile. It was a very lonesome invader at first, and had for its stations the curious towns of the prairie dogs, whose protest against the infringement of the rights of the most ancient form of Squatter Sovereignty are said to have been as vigorous, if as ineffectual, as more intelligent efforts have been since. The coyotes added their united voice to the popular clamor of a vast region that is now checkered with hedgerows, and green with orchards, and dotted with farm-houses.

By its own estimation, the Santa Fe railroad courageously and quickly transformed the desert. It then turned its attention to transforming sites into destination resorts, most significantly the Las Vegas Hot Springs into the ultimate garden and vacation spot. While historian Frederick Jackson Turner metaphorically characterized the West as having "bathing and rejuvenating qualities," the Santa Fe railroad applied these concepts literally as it gave birth to the Montezuma, crown jewel of the Santa Fe system, at the Las Vegas Hot Springs.

The Santa Fe, of course, was not the first to discover the hot springs. Lore has it that over the centuries before the Spanish arrived, the Indians used the springs as a gathering spot and mysterious place of worship. From the founding of Las Vegas in 1835 by Spanish colonists, settlers and travelers enjoyed Los Ojos Calientes, the Hot Springs, located six miles north of Las Vegas in the foothills of the Sangre de Cristo Mountains, just at the opening of the Gallinas Canyon.

The first Anglos to commercially exploit the hot springs were Julian and Antonio Donaldson who were granted the property in 1840 by the Mexican government's local authority. In 1846, the United States Army, having just claimed New Mexico and based at nearby Fort Union, took over the hot springs property and built a hospital for its soldiers. According to an 1890 story on the hot springs in *Harper's Weekly*, this hospital was built like "a long one-story adobe house, fronted by a veranda with posts of natural logs." The army maintained the hospital until 1862, when it was sold and converted to the Adobe Hotel. The most notorious guests at the Adobe Hotel were outlaws Jesse James and Billy the Kid who dined together there on July 27, 1879. The recent arrival of the railroad apparently attracted all types of personalities to Las Vegas and its nearby hot springs.

Among those attracted to the area were Eastern entrepreneurs who saw the potential of the hot springs. A syndicate led by Boston capitalist Alden Speare purchased the property in 1879 and built a new hotel near the old Adobe Hotel. The Hot Springs Hotel, later to be known as the Old Stone Hotel (because of its native sandstone material), opened in December 1879. The Las Vegas paper described it as being "three stories high, supplied with a large dining room, kitchens, parlors, reading rooms, forty or fifty sleeping rooms." It wasn't long before the Santa Fe railroad, which had arrived in nearby Las Vegas that same year, saw the potential of monopolizing the development of the hot springs property itself. In 1880, the railroad created the Las Vegas Hot Springs Company through which it purchased the existing hotel and surrounding property.

The Santa Fe then drew up plans to build an expansive world-class resort hotel and connect it to the main railroad line with a spur line between Las Vegas and the hot springs. The architectural firm of Jerome, Rice, Moore and Emory of Kansas City was commissioned to design the new 270-room luxury resort hotel, which took 15 months to build at a cost of $200,000. It was named the Montezuma, and opened, as did the spur line, in April 1882. The name Montezuma invoked the legendary founder of the Aztec Empire, adding to the mythical character of the hot springs.

A rustic, rambling and expansive structure, the Montezuma was built exclusively of wood and its interior

Hot Springs (or Stone) Hotel, February 1884

Las Vegas Hot Springs, NM

Courtesy of Museum of New Mexico, Neg. No. 102135

Montezuma Hotel, circa 1881-84

Las Vegas Hot Springs, NM

Courtesy of Museum of New Mexico, Neg. No. 86964

was filled with the most modern conveniences of the Victorian era to attract and accommodate affluent tourists from the East. Its design was typical of the large resort hotels of the era built elsewhere in North America. The Montezuma's verandas, towers, dormers and stained glass were all typical of the Queen Anne style of the time but previously unheard of in New Mexico. The magnificence of the structure and the opulence of its style made it unique in New Mexico.

While the Montezuma boasted modern fire-fighting apparatus – fire plugs, hose-reel attachments and water piped to every floor – it nonetheless burnt to the ground on a cold winter night in January 1884, apparently due to a clogged gas line. With so much already invested and the expectation of increasing its passenger load, the Santa Fe railroad immediately announced plans to rebuild the Montezuma in an even larger and more glorious fashion. It engaged the famous Chicago architectural team of Burnham and Root to design a new Montezuma.

Daniel Burnham came from Chicago to assess the situation in person. He determined that the original Montezuma had been poorly sited on the lowlands near the Gallinas River and the adjacent hot springs. The hotel's original location, Burnham felt, deprived guests of the abundant sunlight and country views that could be obtained higher up. The new Montezuma was therefore to be placed on what was known as Reservoir Hill, helping also to make it "absolutely fireproof." Burnham returned to Chicago with these basic ideas and his partner John Root, having never visited the site, completed the design. Roots' biographer described the allure of the Montezuma: "Here the long low building seems to grow out of the very rocks from which its wide projecting roof slants upward. The generous welcome it offers, the sense of shelter from invading storms, the absolute fitness of every line and feature of it, make this far-away inn one of the most exquisite idyls (sic) its author ever dreamed."

Completed in 1885 at a cost of $300,000 the second Montezuma made even more dramatic Victorian statements than its predecessor through its gables, towers, verandas, dormers, bay windows and exterior materials.

Quarry-faced reddish-brown sandstone of the area adorned the exterior of the first two floors, with the upper floors faced with red slate shingles. The interior had a comfortable yet luxurious atmosphere, typified by the wood-paneled entrance lobby as described on the hotel's opening day by the Las Vegas paper:

The finish of the room is white ash, hand rubbed and highly polished, giving a light and cheerful effect. The floor is closely laid in ash, the walls are in elegant hand-carved panels and the ceiling is girded with massive ashen timbers between which is a pretty series of panels all in the prevailing material of the house's interior finish white ash. At the left and opposite the counter is an immense maroon colored terra cotta fireplace made from a special design by Andrews & Co., Chicago. It is in Queen Anne style fully fifteen feet wide and eight feet high. An imposing dormer of cathedral design surmounts the work. The furniture of the office was specially built by Charles L. Page & Co. and consists of heavy lobby chairs in leather upholstery and a long settee to match.

The warmth and hospitality of the Montezuma lobby was reflected as well in the large 60-foot by 100-foot dining room and the more modest, homelike parlors throughout the building.

In addition to having the national reputation of Burnham and Root to promote, the Santa Fe railroad ensured that the second Montezuma had the best fire protection available. Fire plugs and hose reels were installed in every hall. The reservoir was enlarged to provide greater water volume and pressure. Each room had fire alarms connected to a central system. It was the first building in New Mexico lit by electricity, generated in its own plant and delivered throughout the hotel with insulated wiring. The plaster was even said to be fireproof. All this was for naught, however, as only four months after the opening of the second Montezuma, it was engulfed in flames on the night of August 8, 1885. While the alarm had sounded, efforts to extinguish the fire were inhibited by the hoses being far too short to stretch from their reels in the hallway to the tower area where the fire started. Fortunately, no lives were lost but the Montezuma was again destroyed, leaving only burnt timbers and the sandstone shell of the lower floors.

The Santa Fe railroad decided immediately to rebuild, this time virtually duplicating the Burnham and Root design with only subtle changes. It took a year to rebuild the third Montezuma, which opened on August 16, 1886 as the Phoenix Hotel, so named to evoke an image of the mythical bird's resurgence from its own ashes. While the new name was clever and even appropriate, it quickly became evident that it contradicted the appealing image that the Santa Fe railroad sought to promote. The name Phoenix served only as a reminder of the two previous disasters, so after a few months the former name Montezuma was re-adopted.

Having built, rebuilt and again rebuilt the Montezuma, the Santa Fe railroad had a tremendous amount invested in the destination resort. Its passenger department published a promotional booklet in 1887 with hopes of bringing some return on this investment. The prose of this booklet portrays the place – the location of the hot springs in particular and the West in general – in idyllic, mythic terms: "The place itself is a dell, a vale set round on three sides with mountains, a Cyclopean sea-shell with notched edges. It is such a place as, judging from precedent very celebrated, would have been chosen, in the days when feudalism had its choice of all things, for a Baron's Castle."

The authors of the booklet were also well aware of the competition of Southeastern coastal resorts and they did their best to distinguish the benefits of the Montezuma's climate. "But there is utterly lacking the languor of the palm. Some people complain of what they call a certain 'stickiness' of Florida – a warmth without exhilaration – a certain dreamy dread of the hovering mosquito, and a vague feeling that one must fan oneself or perish. This is the bane of the southern coast-resorts. You cannot have the sea and eight thousand feet of elevation at one place and the same time. One must choose between the two."

In spite of all this investment and promotion, the Montezuma was never profitable. In the early 1890s the Montezuma was attracting approximately 18,000 guests a year, which amounts to only 50 per day. Estimates suggest that the hotel was losing $40,000 per year and that the railroad's directors, in spite of their persistence and commitment in the 1880s, were becoming apprehensive of further investment in the 1890s.

Bath House, Montezuma Hotel, circa 1886

Courtesy Citizens Committee for Historic Preservation, Las Vegas, New Mexico,

Photograph No. 1208, CCHP # 2004-5

ERB Collection, Methodist Church

Montezuma Hotel after fire, August 8, 1885

Las Vegas Hot Springs, NM

Courtesy of Museum of New Mexico, Neg. No. 121216

Things got dramatically worse with the nationwide Panic of 1893, an economic crisis that put many business-es, including several railroads, into receivership. The Santa Fe railroad was facing bankruptcy and could no longer sustain the Montezuma.

The Montezuma closed September 1, 1893 – only to reopen for the summer season over the next decade. In spite of renewed efforts, including building an adjacent casino, the Montezuma did not attract the resort traffic. Instead, people were drawn to the greater glamour and spectacle of the Grand Canyon. October 31, 1903, was the Montezuma's last night.

Economic reality finally overtook the romance and persistence of the Montezuma.

In 1882, on the occasion of the opening of the first Montezuma, the Las Vegas paper ran an editorial with this rosy forecast: "The future of Las Vegas, New Mexico, as a great city, is very bright, and no other point in New Mexico will compete with her . . . . There must be some place for men of wealth to live, where conven-iences and luxuries can be had, and Las Vegas is and will be the place." These hopes and expectations, like those held by the Santa Fe railroad for the Montezuma throughout its various incarnations, were dashed.

The Montezuma had tried but failed to be what historian Frederick Jackson Turner had called the West: a magic fountain of youth in which America continually bathed and rejuvenated itself. As much as the Santa Fe railroad depicted the Montezuma as a symbol of the West, the hotel never fulfilled its mythical promise.

Yet, as long as the building has stood throughout the 20th century and now into the 21st century, it has continued to convey its mythical character.

'Mid mountains of New Mexico
Our Montezuma stands,
Unique, sublime and gloriously
Outstretched her beckoning hands
A precious gift to the Glorious West
Hallowed and blest
Her castle wall a beacon bright
Arouse and call for the best.
— *Motto of the Montezuma Baptist College*

Col. Theodore Roosevelt, Rough Rider, circa 1898

Courtesy of Museum of New Mexico, Neg. No. 108210

PARADE OF CELEBRITIES MAKE MONTEZUMA PILGRIMAGE

BY JON BOWMAN

Could one of most notorious outlaws of the Wild West help lay to rest the specter of international terrorism and outlawry looming as pressing issues for the 21st century? The answer is a definitive "yes" if the new Bartos Institute for the Constructive Engagement of Conflict assumes its intended role bringing together diverse world leaders and thinkers to iron out and moderate our most wrenching global conflicts.

What's an outlaw got to do with the Bartos Institute?

The connection is simple – even more clear-cut than the Six Degrees of Separation linking Kevin Bacon to everyone else in the Hollywood firmament. Think in terms of that old ditty: "The hip bone is connected to the thigh bone...."

Ponder this pedigree. The Bartos Institute is the centerpiece of the Montezuma Castle, the newly renovated, one-time luxury resort outside Las Vegas, New Mexico. The Montezuma Castle is the successor to the old Adobe Hotel. It's the first inn on the premises, established by W. Scott Moore, a Missouri-born entrepreneur, to provide lodging alongside the area's soothing hot springs. Now, this is where a legendary bandit enters the picture.

As far as can be verified using the extant hotel ledgers in the possession of the New Mexico State Records Center and Archives, the first "celebrity" of note to stay at the Adobe Hotel was Jesse James, Moore's boyhood buddy from their Missouri days. Of course, all kinds of apocryphal reports have circulated about the Aztec emperor Montezuma dipping his toes in the hot springs (hence the Montezuma monicker attached to the castle). Some have also asserted that on one of his frequent forays into Las Vegas, Billy the Kid might have sampled the curative powers of the springs ahead of Jesse James. Establishing respective bragging rights for frontier gunmen is always a difficult task. But notch this one up for James. He staked out the most long-lasting link to the Montezuma region by signing his John Hancock to the guest register of the Adobe Hotel for a short stay from July 26-29, 1879. According to subsequent reports, James visited at Moore's invitation and came close to arriving at a decision to retire in the vicinity. Who knows if he could have holed up for long at the Adobe Hotel, eluding the treachery of Robert Ford, but we do know he enjoyed his brief respite and spread the word about this hole-in-the-wall place he had discovered.

Many prominent Midwesterners heeded the call, filling the rooms at the Adobe Hotel and its more luxurious successors, the Las Vegas Hot Springs Hotel, the Montezuma Hot Springs Hotel and the Phoenix Hotel. Scions of commerce and industry from Kansas City, St. Louis, Chicago, Cincinnati and Denver represented the first vanguard to join New Mexicans and Texans in vacationing at this pristine

THE RICH
• • • • • •
& FAMOUS

getaway on the westernmost edge of the Great Plains — the so-called "Karlsbad of the New World." Later came fresh waves of well-heeled visitors from New York, Boston and the East Coast, as well as Europe and Asia.

These guests extended their stays far longer than Jesse James — often lingering for months on end — and didn't travel nearly as light. The railroad afforded them the opportunity to pack trunks full of clothing and jewelry, photographs, trinkets and books, everything they could possibly need, including a stash of libations to supplement the Montezuma's well-stocked wine cellars. In a devastating inferno that brought down the original Montezuma hotel on January 8, 1884, volunteer firefighters concentrated on saving the wine cellars. No one bothered to rescue the birds and animals in the Southwest's finest aviary and menagerie. In his wonderful 1960 chapbook *The Montezuma Hot Springs Hotel*, Milton W. Callen noted, "It was jokingly reported that enough liquor was 'liquidated' at the scene of the fire to have quenched the blaze had it been properly applied."

The 60-plus guests then in residence weren't laughing — they lost an estimated $200,000 in jewelry, personal effects, banknotes and clothing, leaving them "bare-headed" and bereft of "a semblance of wraps of any kind," the *Las Vegas Optic* newspaper reported.

Just as it served as the engine promoting tourism across the Southwest, the Santa Fe Railway spurred the popularity of the Montezuma, recruiting 54 employees from the finest hotels back East and banging the drum to extol the resort's virtues in ways that packed a lot more bang than Jesse James' six-shooters. In 1883, in a bold stroke of marketing genius, the railway invited about 75 freight agents on a junket to Mexico, culminating with a sojourn at Montezuma. George W. Street, one of the guests, recorded his impressions in an article he called "Che Wah Wah."

"Adjectives fail to express the excellence of the dinner, or the enjoyment of the entire affair by the gentlemen comprising this party; they doubtless wouldwillingly have remained three hours at the table instead of half that time, had it not been for the necessity of clearing the room for another entertainment to be given in their honor, in the shape of a 'hop.'

"…For three hours the gallant Freight Men were wafted through the intricacies of quadrilles, lanciers and Virginia reels, or revolved in the dizzy whirl of the waltz, with as fair partners as ever graced a ball-room. There were belles from Chicago, Cincinnati, New York, Boston, Pueblo and Las Vegas. At about two o'clock, the orchestra played 'Home Sweet Home' and as the fair guests passed from the ball-room, the 'Montezuma Ideals' sang 'Good Night Ladies'…"

Street also offered a detailed description of the bathhouse experience at the resort's mineral spas. "After disrobing in the quarters assigned to you, a clear-skinned but rather scantily attired attendant makes his appearance, covers you with a sheet, and leads you to a marbled-floored room in which a row of cupboards runs along on one side, from which steam emerges at every chink. Projecting from the top of each of two cupboards you observe a human head, and your blood curdles as the thought flashes through your mind that they may have set up a `Blue Beard' business on you, to make a valuable vacancy in a high official railroad position down East…."

It cost 50 cents for a tub bath, 75 cents to get a tub bath with a vapor treatment and shower, and $1 to receive the full nine yards, including a shampoo, manicure, and "medicated and mercurial" treatments. There was no extra charge for soap, towels or the services of attendants. In an article carried in the June 28, 1890, edition of *Harper's Weekly*, Clarence Pullen compared the alkaline water bubbling up from the 40-odd hot springs to the waters of Toplitz in Austria, "while in the two chief active constituents – the carbonate and sulphate of soda – they much resemble the Carlsbad (Karlsbad in the Czech Republic) waters, but are weaker." A soak in the springs was reputed to cure disorders ranging from chronic rheumatism and gout to renal calculi and dyspepsia.

The main attractions might have been dancing and dining, lounging around in easy chairs on the veranda or baking like a lobster in the bluish-colored waters of the hot springs (the tinge reflecting minute traces of lithium). But the railway provided guests with many other recreational options, including opportunities to gamble in a maze of private card rooms or a massive casino accommodating crowds of up to 1,000. Women could retire to sewing rooms, described in florid terms in an account published by the Globe Printing Company of Las Vegas: "In the upper stories are the sewing rooms, where the Misses Grundy can do considerable work, while the numerous caged birds do their warbling and the maiden plants put forth their rarest flowers and shed their refreshing odors in the mellow light that comes streaming through the stained windows."

Men, meanwhile, could rub elbows while descending in an elevator down to the basement where "provision has been made for the hardier sex. There are billiard parlors and bowling alleys [the first west of the Mississippi], all finished in the native pine." To keep these subterranean game rooms well lit, the Montezuma boasted the first electrical wiring ever installed in New Mexico. The most opulent in furnishings – carved out of exotic woods including cocobolo, ebony and French walnut – graced the hotel rooms. The large fireplace in the lobby, crafted by a French artisan, reached upward for three stories. But it wasn't the indoor fixtures that lured Easterners to the Montezuma so much as the opportunity to sample the rugged, wide-open spaces of West while basking in the lap of luxury. It was no accident that such robust adventurers as Teddy Roosevelt (then governor of New York) and Ulysses S. Grant (at the time an Army general) joined the pilgrimage to the Montezuma.

Elaborate topiary gardens abutted the hotel and a flanking plaza provided facilities for archery, lawn tennis, croquet and cricket. Guests also could sign on for longer treks into the Sangre de Cristo Mountains outside Mora and Pecos. The itinerary for women usually included picnics in the woods and day-long burro riding trips. "Every morning a train of these sure-footed, docile, little animals is brought before the door in waiting for the riding parties," *Harper's Weekly* related. "…The spectacle of a burro subsiding beneath the weight of a stout lady, and settling himself comfortably on the ground, with a total dismissal of all idea of rising, is not uncommon in these excursions." While the women wrestled with the burros, the menfolk could freely vanish for two or three days, hunting deer, elk, antelope, wild turkeys, black bears, grizzlies and mountain lions.

Anyone longing for the citified comforts of home needed only retreat to Las Vegas, then the commercial hub and largest metropolis in the New Mexico Territory. The city of about 8,000 supported the popular Tamme Opera House, numerous bars hawking genuine Milwaukee beer and a professional baseball team that went to bat against "the Bully Boys from Albuquerque," as well as an archrival team from Santa Fe. Not only did divas hold forth at the opera house, but the *Optic* recorded a special appearance in 1886 by a troupe of Japanese acrobats and singers "direct from the Court Theatre of his Majesty, the Mikado of Japan." The troupe presented a separate performance for Las Vegas' large resident Chinese population, men who had built the railroads or ran laundries in town.

The *Optic* waxed eloquent, portraying Las Vegas as a progressive city on the move, embracing the latest accoutrements of culture and refinement, and distancing itself from its more rough-and-tumble frontier origins. One of the paper's most glowing puff pieces boasted that Las Vegas could claim "the purest water in the land and a…system of waterworks, banking facilities, daily newspapers, street railways, telephone exchange, gas works, nine new railroads, etc. … Good quarries are all around us containing rock of almost every hue. Red, white and blue are the prominent colors."

Still, wild anecdotes crept into the back pages of the *Optic*. According to one such entry, "There was a report about town today that Capt. J.W. Barney had been killed in a railway accident near Columbus. The name of the man who was killed was Barney Bollinger. Anyone starting such a rumor should be held under a pump for half an hour." With tongue-in-cheek aplomb, an 1886 filler declared, "A man is traveling through Texas claiming to be the Lord. He is believed to be an imposter."

If the Lord had ventured west to Montezuma, he would have been in good company. Anybody who was anyone checked into the lobby — not only to relax and unwind, but also to be seen and to establish one's high standing in the social pecking order. President Rutherford B. Hayes put in an appearance. So did famed Civil War Gen. William Tecumseh Sherman and the explorer John Fremont. Royal visitors included the Marquis of Lorne and Princess Louise, Queen Victoria's daughter. In an interesting footnote, the Duke of Rutland from Great Britain stopped off at Montezuma with his wife while touring the United States. Wishing to experience a truly Western-style adventure, they took meals at the hotel, but camped outside on the grounds. One small complication eventually forced them indoors — the birth in 1882 of their eldest daughter, sibling to Lady Diana Manners, the famous actress. (The first birth on the premises had actually come a few months earlier in the spring of 1882 as Mr. and Mrs. J.W. Brewster of Howard, Kansas, had a baby girl — an occasion celebrated in George W. Price's short-lived *Montezuma Courier*.

Perhaps the largest contingent of guests arrived in 1888 when the Oddfellows Lodge staged its national convention in Las Vegas, commissioning two trains to bring the approximately 1,000 delegates to the Montezuma. The *Daily Optic*, the Las Vegas mayor and civic leaders encouraged an all-out effort on the part of residents to serve as escorts. "The main part is to show them as much of the town as possible before they visit the springs," the *Optic* reported. All the showcasing went for naught. Both Las Vegas and the Montezuma got blindsided in the 1890s by a nationwide economic tailspin and the opening of many competitive resorts across the West, including El Tovar at the Grand Canyon.

By 1904, the hotel had closed its doors — its parade of celebrities replaced by students from the Montezuma Baptist College and, following 1937, Mexican seminarians studying for the priesthood who could not pursue their religious training at home without facing reprisals from Mexico's anticlerical government. For a few months in 1912, the Montezuma grabbed headlines and reclaimed a glimmer of its former grandeur when boxer Jim Flynn chose the abandoned hotel as the training camp for his much-ballyhooed world championship bout with Jack Johnson in Las Vegas on July 4, 1912 (this prize fight became the subject of the movie *The Great White Hope*).

Industrialist Armand Hammer's decision to purchase the castle and surroundings grounds — working in close cooperation with Prince Charles, Queen Noor Al-Hussein of Jordan and others to create an American campus of the United World College — brought a whole new generation of celebrities to Montezuma. Since the 1982 opening of the college, Malcolm Forbes of *Forbes Magazine* has dropped by, as well as columnist Ann Landers, composer Philip Glass, singer and songwriter Judy Collins, French-Canadian astronaut Julie Payette, Nokia President and CEO Jorma Ollila and Abiodun Williams, advisor to the United Nations Secretary General.

Dignitaries packed the premises for the first public unveiling of the castle's renovation, a colorful celebration on September 29, 2001, presided over by Queen Noor. Crown Prince Pavlos of Greece shared the limelight, returning to his alma mater after a 15-year absence. Shelby Davis, the globally minded philanthropist who endowed much of the project, beamed as he accepted an outpouring of gratitude from United World College students representing 83 nations and dressed in their traditional costumes.
The eloquence flowed freely inside the sparkling halls. New Mexico Governor Gary Johnson and former United Nations Ambassador Bill Richardson, among others, addressed the castle's historical and architectural significance, as well as its newfound importance housing an institute designed to foster global understanding and to help feuding parties and governments resolve their disputes amicably.

But the charismatic Queen Noor best captured the awe of the 500 well-wishers in attendance. "I never could have dreamed that this castle would arise out of the dilapidated ruins that I saw years ago on my first visit to this campus," she said. "I am proud and encouraged by the good use that will be made of these premises, and hopeful that the world will become a better place as a result."

Montezuma Hotel

Las Vegas Hot Springs, NM

Courtesy of Museum of New Mexico, Neg. No. 170730

EAST MEETS WEST AGAINST EYE-DROPPING LUXURY
BY HEIDI UTZ

During the Gilded Age of the late 1800s, a new industrial society gave rise to an unprecedented number of American millionaires with time, money and the desire to flaunt it. Business tycoons, socialites, fortune-hunters, politicos and rogues spent their leisure hours soaking in spas and luxuriating at lavish resorts in decadent comfort.

This age of excess stemmed in part from the explosive development of the railroad, which not only spawned a generation of new millionaires and allowed them to travel cross-country, but also transported goods from far away to luxury resorts. Around 1880, railroad owners began marketing the Pullman palace car, a well-appointed "hotel on wheels" that made first-class travel available to anyone who could afford its comforts. In response, a devoted following enthusiastically embraced the "wild frontier" from the vantage point of their own cushioned seats.

Soon the ease and excitement of railroad travel, combined with the leisure class' newfound wanderlust, led to another development: the modern grand resort. As Easterners' fascination with the West was piqued, railroad companies specially designed "destination resorts," vacation spots along their lines that would create a symbiotic relationship between rail and hotel. Business boomed.

Because urbanites fancied themselves rugged explorers of virgin territory, resort developers sought to situate their properties in naturally appealing settings—while, of course, providing luxurious accommodations. This dichotomy extended to resort grounds, where hoteliers maintained elegantly manicured gardens often in marked contrast to the natural landscape. Sometimes the staff even cultivated a faux-wilderness setting to play up the notion of the resort as safe harbor from the surrounding "wilds."

RESORT FIT FOR ROYALTY

Landscape often provided the resort's *raison d'être*, with accommodations frequently situated on or near such natural splendors as mineral springs, beaches or waterfalls. These establishments' popularity was part of America's growing appreciation for the natural world, as demonstrated by the 1872 establishment of Yellowstone as our first national park. But the park's immediate construction of first-class lodgings proved that not every vacationer desired a rugged experience.

Indeed, Western resort owners prided themselves in providing all of the services available at contemporary urban hotels back East, including up-to-the-minute appliances, technology and indulgences. Handpicking their staffs from top New York, Chicago and St. Louis hotels, they strove to meet their patrons' lofty standards in recreation, ambience and cuisine.

Among those who became increasingly fascinated with the mysteries west of the Mississippi were prominent business magnates, diplomats, presidents and generals. Indeed, anyone who was "anyone" found his or her way to the West's most distinguished resort: the Montezuma Hotel.

Looming like a storybook castle in the distance, this Queen Anne-style colossus sprung from the eastern foothills of the Sangre de Cristo Mountains of northern New Mexico. First developed in 1882 by the Atchison, Topeka & Santa Fe Railway (which had driven its first spike into New Mexican soil three years prior), this "destination resort" catered to the needs and whims of an elite clientele. Sited just off the main rail line to Southern California, it lay about 70 miles from Santa Fe and minutes from the New Mexico boomtown of Las Vegas.

For a clientele seeking "uncharted wilderness," what better place than the pre-statehood territory of northern New Mexico. To the city slicker, this sparsely populated, mountainous, high-desert region with its singular geology must have seemed like the ends of the earth. At the Montezuma, guests could spend their days exploring the hotel area's natural beauty, fishing for trout in nearby Gallinas Canyon, strolling the property's 100-acre grounds and, of course, lolling in one of 40 mineral springs.

These were some of the continent's most celebrated hot springs, nationally renowned for their curative powers. The infirm came here to get well; the healthy, simply to enjoy themselves. In fact, according to Las Vegas newspaper *The Optic*, the area was considered a "natural sanatorium … combining more natural advantages than any other place in America … Her thermal waters are the equal of the Hot Springs of Arkansas, while her climate is indefinitely superior … The air is pure, dry rarified and highly electrified—a certain cure for consumption, if the disease be taken in time."

Health was considered a popular excuse to get away, with a change of scenery deemed vital to both mind and body. Since colonial times, Americans had visited mineral springs to renew their health or find spiritual enlightenment, aesthetic catharsis or simple relaxation. They later came to regard as salubrious the springs' accompanying hotels, since they admitted plenty of light and air while providing easy access from their public spaces to the verandas and gardens. At the Montezuma, guests could take their daily constitutional through a park landscaped with broad bluegrass lawns, rare flowers, shade trees, gravel walkways and a large central fountain.

The hotel first opened its doors on April 17, 1882. The $200,000 structure was larger, more opulent and more up-to-date than any comparable building in the state. Boasting three stories and 270 rooms, it featured every modern convenience with posh appointments from New York, Boston, and Kansas City that made urbanites feel right at home. Amenities extended to gaslight, steam heat and water piped to every floor, while the kitchen was stocked with refrigerators, ranges, broilers and even a revolving steam wringer and cylinder washing machine. Though few American homes had yet adopted them, such innovations were not unusual in 19th-century's grand resorts.

Designed in the era's beloved Queen Anne style, the Montezuma coupled classical and anticlassical motifs with a rustic exterior. The hotel's original architect remains unknown, but he's likely to have been a New Mexico newcomer who previously practiced in a Midwest city. His architecturally modern creation was unique in an area in which Territorial adobes were still popular. No doubt, its whimsical, picturesque style helped the building stand out as a fantasy, embodying all the dreams that Easterners looked toward the West to fulfill. It was quickly dubbed "the Castle."

While unusual for New Mexico, the Montezuma's architectural elements — including dormers, long verandas, latticed balconies and multipaned stained glass windows — well represented the era's Western-resort architecture. Such buildings were designed to blend organically with their surroundings and to provide comfortable yet rustic Rocky Mountain charm. Long and informally rambling, they projected the breezy, carefree environment of beach, country or mountain vacations.

Though resort architects incorporated extensive precautions into their designs, in the late 19th century, fire still represented a major threat to hotels. In January 1884, the Montezuma's gas mains became clogged, burning the building to the ground. Unfazed, the Santa Fe Railway almost immediately planned an even grander resort, to be designed by prominent Chicago architects Burnham and Root.

John Root never set foot on the hotel's site, but relying on Daniel Burnham's reports, he effectively conceived a structure that combined Eastern efficiency and sophistication with a sensitivity to the landscape. According to Root's biographer, Harriet Moore, "The long, low building seems to grow out of the very rocks from which its wide projecting roof slants upward."

Unveiled on April 20, 1885, the 90,000-square-foot resort featured the day's finest amenities. Faced in the area's reddish-brown sandstone, the four-story structure sat atop Reservoir Hill, several hundred feet above a river basin, providing a magnificent view of Gallinas Canyon. Root had sited the hotel so that sunlight streamed through its windows and showed off the building to its full advantage.

Though its architect generally disdained the frivolity of the Queen Anne style, preferring instead that form more closely follow function, the Montezuma's design was once again distinctly Queen Anne. (While vacationers favored such picturesque styles, architects sometimes regarded them as merely eclectic novelties sporting useless, arbitrary forms.) In planning his castle, Root made certain that the varied decorative elements worked together to produce design unity as well as visual and textural interest. Relatively simple yet never severe in its detail, the resort appeared at once rustic and sophisticated, comfortable and homey.

Root stressed colors found in nature, warm reds and browns that nicely contrasted with the area's brilliant blue sky. These tones, along with the hotel's low, rambling quality, made it an excellent example of organic architecture. Like New Mexican adobes, the structure did not intrude on its natural surroundings, but instead seemed to shoot up from the hillside. Dull red shingles on its upper story and towers, the light trim and a roof faced with gray slate lent it both rich color and subtle tone.

The second Montezuma resembled its predecessor in its complex, asymmetrical form. However, the architect did change it considerably, modifying roof direction, gables, towers, verandas, dormers and windows, and adding three onion-capped towers, each of different profile and height. Root played with many varieties of window, from bay to arched, which combined with the towers to form a harmonious, visually interesting composition. One of the building's most outstanding features was an immense, 330-foot-long, 18-foot-wide, balustraded wooden veranda that wrapped around its west, south and east facades. Such prominent porches were a specifically American addition to the Queen Anne style.

Inside, the hotel maintained a comfortable yet luxurious atmosphere typical of Queen Anne- and Shingle-style interiors. Its basically L-shaped plan was long and narrow, with no more than two rooms separated by a corridor placed back-to-back. Walking through the front door, guests were struck with its vast, wood-paneled entrance hall and long, ornately carved reception desk. This lobby/office exemplified the late-19th-century Queen Anne entrance hall.

Lobby furnishings were also typically Queen Anne in their abundant displays of carving, turning and

Montezuma Hotel lobby and main lobby
circa 1887
Las Vegas Hot Springs, NM
Courtesy of Museum of New Mexico
Neg. No. 122069

leather paneling. Exceptions were plantlike, Art Nouveau-style light fixtures and an immense Gothic Revival, maroon terra cotta fireplace. The entrance hall was finished in white ash, hand-rubbed and highly polished for a light and cheerful effect, while wood paneling and stained glass lent it warmth and hospitality. Root may have denigrated the Queen Anne style, but he'd certainly mastered its implementation.

Less complex in detail were the hotel's parlors, which had a domestic feel enhanced by their majestic Queen Anne fireplaces. The main dining room was also a homey Queen Anne, containing a wood-beamed, bracketed ceiling and a planked floor. Simple, utilitarian chairs surrounded 36 ash tables, while stained-glass windows and Art Nouveau chandeliers contributed light and charm. But guests undoubtedly were most impressed with the room's centerpiece: a massive buffet embellished with huge stained-glass panels and a 3-foot-by-10-foot oblong French mirror.

The Montezuma's kitchen was predictably well equipped, featuring up-to-the-minute appliances, its own bakery (catering to railroad restaurants from New Mexico to the Grand Canyon), and a cuisine expertly directed by Santa Fe concessionaire Fred Harvey. Nicknamed the "Lucullus of the West," Harvey's excellent food and courteous service matched that of most Eastern restaurants. Dishes served ranged from high quality to occasionally exotic. Harvey even convinced a Yaqui Indian tribe to ship him live green turtles and sea celery from the Gulf of Lower California. Turtles swam in a specially designed pool until they were needed for steaks and the chef's delicious green-turtle soup.

If that weren't enough, an 11-lane bowling alley and a miniature zoo of native animals—bear, fox, owls and deer—added to the resort's charms (though not to its cuisine).

The Montezuma bustled with patrons, including the likes of Ulysses S. Grant, Jesse James, and Teddy Roosevelt, until August 9, 1885, when fire struck once again. Although Root had planned the building to be "absolutely fireproof" and had taken every possible precaution, the massive structure again burned almost completely to the ground.

A year later, the place again rose from the ashes, as the aptly named Phoenix Hotel (though it continued to be known as the Montezuma). A standing seam metal roof replaced its previous gray slate, and the 343-room structure managed to resist fire. This time, however, its nemesis proved to be the changing whims of its wealthy habitués, and after less than a decade, the third Montezuma was forced to close due to competition from other Western resorts.

Two years later, in 1895, the hotel re-opened for the fourth and final time. On the property, new management added a separate building called the Casino, complete with stage, dance floor and resident orchestra. But even those attractions lacked the power to make such a mammoth undertaking financially solvent, and in 1904, the Montezuma permanently closed. The era of the great American resort hotel had ended, and the wealthy moved on to play in the sands of Miami Beach and Palm Springs.

Dining room, Montezuma Hotel, circa 1886

Courtesy Citizens Committee for Historic Preservation, Las Vegas, New Mexico,

Photograph No. 1211, CCHP # 2024-5

ERB Collection, Methodist Church

THE STORY BEHIND AN ARCHITECTURAL FACELIFT
BY NANCY HANKS, PH.D.& MARK THALER, PROJECT ARCHITECT

The process of restoring Montezuma Castle began in earnest in 1997, when the National Trust for Historic Preservation included the building in its list of the Eleven Most Endangered Places. The exposure galvanized efforts aimed at saving the building. Clearly, the Montezuma was of national, as well as regional importance. In 1998, Montezuma Castle was named as one of America's Treasures by the White House Millennium Council, the first structure to be so named west of the Mississippi River.

Later that spring, the United World College (UWC) hired Santa Fe architect Laban Wingert to prepare a feasibility study for the building's reuse. As part of the study, Wingert began to identify functions that could logically be incorporated into the long-vacant structure. This study also addressed renovation issues and a preliminary budget, which helped UWC's planning efforts.

UWC pursued a very deliberate approach in selecting the best architectural firm available to transform the vacant Montezuma Castle into the centerpiece of the campus. The college sent letters to the State Historic Preservation Offices in each of the 50 states asking that they forward the letter to preservation firms they considered qualified to complete the project. From an initial pool of more than 100 interested firms, nine were invited to the campus to see the building and gain a better understanding of the UWC and its goals. After several more meetings and interviews, the firm of Einhorn Yaffee Prescott Architecture & Engineering, PC of Albany, New York (EYP) was selected in April 1999 to complete the project.

THEN

AND NOW

Next came complete measurement, documentation and drawing of all existing conditions found in the 90,000-square foot building. This allowed accurate construction documents and budgets to be developed for the renovation. Teams of EYP architects and engineers spent several months accumulating the necessary information to develop the drawings and specifications. Numerous probes exposed conditions that could not be seen that might affect the piping, ductwork or other hidden aspects of the construction. Nothing was left to chance.

The scope of work included safety-oriented improvements, providing accessibility for the people with disabilities, complete upgrades of mechanical systems, hazardous waste removal, structural stabilization, and restoration and preservation of the building's façade and public areas – all tied to budget and schedule. General contractors were Bradbury Stamm Construction from Albuquerque and the Franken Construction Company, Inc. from Las Vegas, N.M. In all, more than 125 workers assisted with the project, contributing to the cost of about $1 million a month for restoration.

Using a team approach, EYP met with representatives of the New Mexico Construction Industries

Division, New Mexico State Historic Preservation Division and the Governor's Committee on Concerns of the Handicapped to address these issues at the beginning of the design process. Each group shared their respective concerns. Out of this common dialogue, creative solutions emerged that addressed everyone's needs.

The 19th-century layout actually fit well with the adaptive reuse of the building as a school. The ground floor, once a basement with a bowling alley and billiard tables, has been reconstructed to house a student recreation center and bookstore.

The first floor features a large ash and oak wood-paneled lobby that once greeted hotel guests, and is now dedicated to King Hussein of Jordan, for student use. The first floor also houses a dining room, kitchen and guest accommodations in a separate wing intended to serve as adult housing for summer programs, visiting dignitaries and use in the conflict resolution program.

On the second floor, areas that were once hotel sleeping and meeting rooms now contain classrooms, administrative space, student dormitory rooms and faculty apartments. The third floor also has meeting rooms, classrooms and student rooms, with the section over the kitchen sealed off. Another part of the third floor is also sealed off, as is part of the second floor, and the entire fourth floor, all awaiting future growth of UWC.

For Safety's Sake

Architects identified immediate safety issues in the dining room, historically the most spectacular space in Montezuma Castle. As originally built, the building had five trusses over the dining room to support the upper floors. Made from a combination of timber and dimensional lumber with wrought iron tie rods and cast iron joint fittings, these trusses allowed for the dining room's grand 60-foot by 100-foot clearspan space.

By 1938, however, problems with the trusses became evident. At that time, the trusses were reinforced with 7-inch diameter steel shoring columns added under the center of the bottom chord of each of the five 12-foot high by 60-foot wide trusses. This steel shoring ran from the dining room down through the basement, marring more than the aesthetics of the grand dining room. Evidently, during the installation of the shores, the trusses were jacked-up slightly, resulting in reverse curvature of the trusses and pushing out the exterior walls above the dining room. Early in the reconstruction, it became clear that significant failure had occurred at every truss.

The five trusses were literally tearing themselves apart. Reinforcement of the existing structure was ruled out as an option due to the variable conditions from truss to truss and the inherent difficulties of reinforcing the bolted connections. Instead, a scheme was devised by EYP to install pairs of steel trusses that would sandwich the timber trusses. All floor and roof loads would be directly transferred to the new

Parlor, Montezuma Hotel, circa 1886
Courtesy Citizens Committee for Historic Preservation
Las Vegas, New Mexico,
Photograph No. 1215, CCHP # 2030-31
ERB Collection, Methodist Church

Bedroom at the Montezuma Hotel, circa 1886
A rare view of the Montezuma interior.
Courtesy Citizens Committee for Historic Preservation
Las Vegas, New Mexico,
Photograph No. 1201, CCHP # 2018
ERB Collection, Methodist Church

steel structure, while leaving the old trusses in place. In order to accomplish this, the building had to be jacked up five and three-eighths inches from the bottom, so that the original beams could be reached and steel reinforcement bolted around them on the second floor. It took three weeks to raise the second floor just one inch through the use of shoring towers and jacking beams.

However difficult, this accomplished the goal of avoiding significant alteration to the architecture of the dining room. The grand space will once again be column-free thanks to the steel trusses concealed overhead. Visitors can view part of one of the trusses, which has been left exposed on the second floor. In addition, two eight-foot glass chandeliers by renowned artist Dale Chihuly have been installed, designed to complement the already existing stained glass and colors in the dining room.

The new dining room will serve approximately 300 students, faculty and staff three meals a day.

Another structural issue lay in the collapse of the brick-bearing walls in the ground floor basement area below the old kitchen, causing the floors above to pitch more than 6 inches. Because of seepage in the stone foundation walls, water literally poured through some of the walls when it rained. In addition, the area had many asbestos-wrapped pipes that had to be removed. Once this was done, the upper floors were temporarily shored. The entire first floor structure was removed and a new concrete slab installed in the kitchen wing to accommodate a modern kitchen.

Serving New Needs for Greater Access

Accessibility had to be integrated into the design of the building to meet the standards of the Americans with Disabilities Act (ADA). Take the old elevator, which was literally central to the Castle. The elevator only served the full floors and not the half levels (as a result of the higher ceiling in the dining room section of the building).

The architects opted to install a new elevator, which does meet ADA requirements, located in the last bay of the dining room, allowing it to serve the two separate wings of the building. This also creates an entry foyer with storage and coatroom facilities for the dining room, and makes the dining room more symmetrical than before. The old elevator has now been enclosed as mechanical space and is used as vertical routing for modern telecommunications wiring.

Improvements That Don't Meet the Eye

Although Montezuma Castle was the first building in New Mexico with electric lights, a completely new electrical system had to be installed, as well as new plumbing, new sprinklers, fire detectors and data/telecommunications connections. The City of Las Vegas extended gas lines so that the Castle could experience gas heating for the first time. Now there are gas boilers on the ground floor level, and new radiators throughout. Each room has individual thermostat controls, but no air conditioning was installed because of the moderate summer climate in the area.

The wiring of the guestrooms was a special challenge due to the limited space between floors. At times, the wiring had to be extended from a room in an upper level down to the basement and back up to another room to assure that there were wall plugs and telephone outlets in each room. In addition, ceilings were lowered about 3 inches to route conduit and sprinkler piping.

RESTORATION AND PRESERVATION

The most historically accurate changes in Montezuma Castle are in the restoration of the façade and public spaces. The building has historically had a "public" face and a "back" face.

The public face, primarily the east and south facades, has ashlar-cut brownstone with red slate cladding above it, while the back facing west and north facades have local sandstone and black slate cladding. Both facades have been restored in kind, with selective repointing to remove and replace any deteriorated mortar.

Veranda at the Montezuma Hotel, circa 1886
Courtesy Citizens Committee for Historic Preservation
Las Vegas, New Mexico,
Photograph No. 1206, CCHP # 2010-11
ERB Collection, Methodist Church

The existing masonry walls have simply been washed. The original double-hung windows have all been restored by Franken, a tribute to the quality of their original virgin growth pine wood composition. The windows have also been weather-stripped, their hardware repaired, sash weights installed, and both sashes and frames repainted their original colors. All windows in the building are now operable.

The original slate roof was replaced with a metal roof in the 1930s, and a metal roof was used for the restoration, both to blend in with the aesthetic of the existing campus buildings and to allow the project to remain within its budget. Those older elements of the 1930s roof that were still usable were donated to the nearby Las Vegas historic preservation group, the Citizens' Committee for Historic Preservation. The new roof is standing seam galvanized metal and the towers were sheathed with metal shingle. In reconstructing the roof, the steep pitch made full body harnesses, tie-off systems and other fall protection devices a requirement for the roofers.

Main fireplace at the Montezuma Hotel, circa 1885
Courtesy Citizens Committee for Historic Preservation,
Las Vegas, New Mexico,
Photograph No. 1212, CCHP # 2026-7
ERB Collection, Methodist Church

The veranda, once a grand place to see and be seen, was originally wrapped around the east, south and west sides of the building, ending at a *porte-cochère* on the east. Prior to the renovation, however, the veranda was dilapidated and ready to collapse. In restoring it, the only modification is a new enclosure at the west end, using some of the storm panels that had been installed as wind breaks on the veranda in the 1920s.

The original veranda floor presented accessibility issues in that it was one step lower than the front door of the Castle. The new veranda floor is a tongue-and-groove (replacing the original tongue-and-groove) installed over a waterproofed concrete slab.

The exterior entrance to the lobby has been redesigned to include a new, visually non-intrusive ADA ramp, which blends with the rest of the entry and leads up to the veranda from the reconstructed porte-cochère . In addition, a "peace garden" has been reconstructed off of the southwestern corner of the veranda.

The interior courtyard was originally a baggage drop-off and a service entrance for hotel, and then a garden space for the Jesuit seminary. All of that was lost to time. The new design mixes both the contemplative garden space of the Jesuits with a space that the students can use for recreation. There are two sunken courtyards, one a lightwell with a ramp overhead connecting the lobby with the interior courtyard. The other sunken courtyard is primarily a light court for the game rooms on the ground floor, and contains a modern sculpture by Catherine Ferrell.

Inside the Castle, the lobby retains its dominance as an elegant public space. Its great fireplace and stained-glass windows over the doors are restored and a new reception desk has been installed, based on the original design. The original woodwork has been cleaned and refinished, including the ceiling, which was a special challenge because of fire safety issues. Instead of taking the wood-coffered ceiling off the lobby, sprinklering was accomplished by taking up the floorboards on the second floor overhead. The grand staircase from the lobby to the second floor was completely rebuilt, due to structural problems and safety issues. All of the old wood elements and railings, however, were reused, and on the staircase – and in all the public spaces – carpeting has been installed to resemble the original.

Certain other interior details have also been restored, including the doors, their transoms and the wall molding, all rehabilitated on site. The window treatments are a combination of original wood shutters on some of the first floor areas and wood or metal blinds in the rest of the building. The color scheme for painting the interior was based on original colors, although simplified since there were so many layers of paint from which to choose. The furniture – while not original – was selected by EYP to complement the interior of the building.

A prime concern for UWC was that Montezuma Castle be usable for educational purposes to house dining, student residential, recreational, administrative, conferencing facilities and the new Bartos Institute for the Constructive Engagement of Conflict. In the end, the renovation of Montezuma Castle has fulfilled the needs of the college, as well as the hopes and dreams of so many who longed to see the building saved.

Untapped: Hidden rooms in the castle await future expansion by the United World College.

Photo: Polly Mullen.

These Vintage American Structures Could Crumble for All Time

By Bette Brodsky

Who can walk through a run-down, abandoned old building and not feel that the forgotten rooms and hallways, slanting light and faded colors, secret chambers and hidden staircases somehow reflect human emotions? Loneliness, age, fears of being cast aside come to the fore, along with remorse for the passing of older values, no longer appreciated. But the anticipation of discovery accompanies the feeling of loss.

Exploring the deserted spaces, we sense the presence of ghosts and feel both fear and wonder as we climb a narrow stairway toward the crack-lit doorway leading to the open tower on the third floor. How many others have walked these halls and enjoyed the view from the veranda?

These bittersweet sensations stoke the passions of architectural preservationists. They are not Luddites — stuck in the past, refusing to see anything good in progress and change — just appreciative of the bedraggled beauty of courtyards cluttered with weeds, volunteer trees and dog-patch-style outbuildings, discarded light fixtures and radiators, and the haunting colors of layers of old paint on time-damaged walls glimpsed through open doorways.

At the same time they love the process of renovation: excavations that reveal rock walls, secret passages, blighted skylights, tunnels and dungeons, attics that resemble the hold of a ship — ribs exposed. They revel in the slow transformation of the rickety and moldy old structure into something else: its look, when halfway done, that hovers between the loveliness and elegance of the old structure and the promise of the new. Will it be better or lose its grandeur? Do we have the skill and the talent to do justice to the memory, so that the new inhabitants will also be able to delight in the discovery of obscure corners and surprising sources of light?

RENOVATION PORTFOLIO

This portfolio of photographs expresses the thrill I felt when I explored the Montezuma castle twice in the company of Polly Mullen, a free-lance photographer who had full access to the construction site and spent 1 1/2 years taking most of the pictures on the following pages. She was my guide through its labyrinthine passages, describing every aspect of the excavation and renovation and introducing me to crew members we met along the way. Only the word "passion" can explain her dedication, persistence, attachment and the scope of her body of work.

Together we sifted through more than 3,000 of her photographs to choose the 100 or so that are published in this portfolio. As you look through the pages I hope you'll feel the mixture of discovery, wonder, loss, appreciation and awe that I did on my tours of the site with Polly.

Hope is the feeling that I get when the new, so expertly done, replaces the old, so lovely and gracious.

Additional photography of the completely renovated castle was done by Chun Y Lai, a New York City based photographer who resides in the lower Hudson Valley hamlet of Garrison, N.Y. with his wife, two boys, two cats and one dog. His work has appeared in numerous books on architecture and design. His magazine credits include *Architectural Record, Interior Design, House + Garden, Contract, Metropolis, VM+SD* and *How*.

41

A room with a view: The castle overlooks a courtyard and a ramshackle cluster of outbuildings.

Photos pages 42 & 43: Polly Mullen.

Diamond in the rough: Before the extensive renovation, the castle courtyard evoked the storied majesty of an abandoned European village.

Back to basics: As part of the restoration process, additions to the structure are removed to reveal the original architecture.

Photos pages 44 & 45: Polly Mullen.

Taking shape: The courtyard begins to suggest its sweep and scale after workers clear away the debris.

Spit polish needed: The castle's old metal roof had lost its luster and required removal of asbestos shingles (seen in the foreground).

Photos pages 46 & 47: Polly Mullen.

Master floor plan: Original planks define the contours of the observation deck in the castle's large turret.

Weather-resistant: Rain, snow, sleet and hail didn't deter progress on the construction site.

Massive makeover: The veranda was completely removed and reconstructed in the early stages of the renovation.

Photos pages 48 & 49: Polly Mullen.

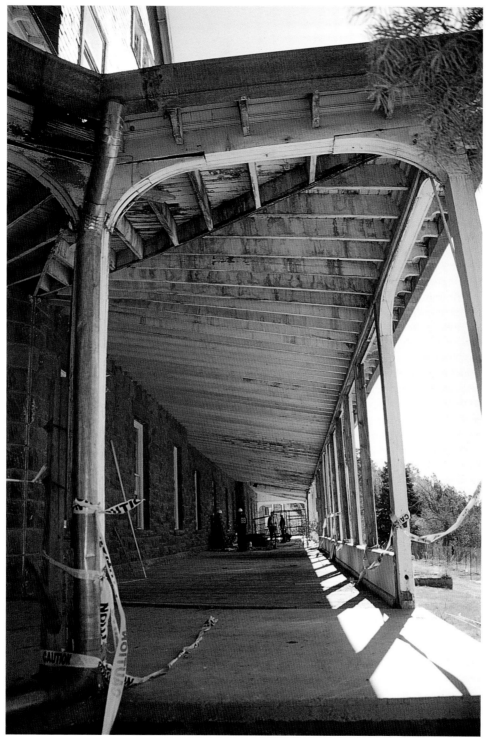

In need of repair: A view of the warped veranda roof before demolition.

From the perch: Light streams through a secret doorway leading to the large tower, pictured at left.

Photos pages 50 & 51: Polly Mullen.

Touching the sky: The castle's west tower also boasts an observation deck, as well as a 5-foot finial, or crowning decorative knob, that had to be rebuilt.

Bringing out the beauty: The castle's elegance came shining through as each stage of the construction neared completion.

Photo: Polly Mullen.

Photo: Chun Y Lai.

Photo: Polly Mullen.

Photo: Chun Y Lai.

Facing a brighter future: The castle rises anew as the renovation wraps in the fall of 2001.

Photo: Chun Y Lai.

THIS PAGE – Taking shape: Wooden frames provide bearing to the sub-floor of the new veranda.

OPPOSITE – Hospitable surroundings: The smoothly curving veranda offers a gracious setting to survey the castle grounds.

Photo: Polly Mullen.

Photo: Chun Y Lai.

Picture-perfect: The arches of the observation tower frame the uplifting natural expanses seen from the Montezuma Castle.

Photos pages 56 & 57: Polly Mullen.

Natural contours: The observation deck (top)
and veranda (bottom) are encircled by pine
forests and rolling hills.

Final touch: A new flagpole caps off the
castle's gleaming metallic roof
Photo: Polly Mullen.

Straight and strong: The new standing seam roof conjures up linear beauty and solidity.

Photo: Chun Y Lai.

WINDOWS

Aerial assault: A crane had to be summoned to haul dilapidated bathtubs and radiators through the castle's wood-frame windows.

Photos pages 60 & 61: Polly Mullen.

Setting the framework: The castle boasts close to 350 windows and 700 sashes. Under the direction of Franken Construction in Las Vegas, a team of 15 laborers worked for 11 months on the Herculean effort to restore the windows.

Detailed artistry: The castle's many exquisite fixtures include the original stained-glass windows above the dining room fireplace (top) and one of the original skylights (below). On the opposite page are a few of the building's arched windows containing colored glass. Replacement panes were painstakingly matched.

Photos pages 62 & 63: Polly Mullen.

Enchanting entrances: Some 400 doors guide visitors into the castle's maze of suites and chambers. Bradbury Stamm Construction Company of Albuquerque restored about half of the original doors, while replacing the rest with authentic replicas.

Photos pages 64 & 65: Polly Mullen.

DOORS

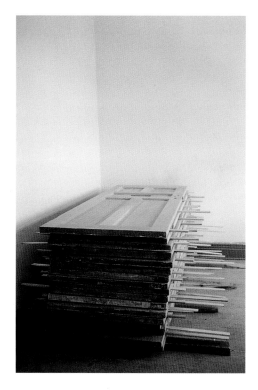

Tunneling down: Site of the first bowling alley west of the Mississippi River, the castle basement had crumbled into disarray. Workers preceded cautiously into the subterranean depths, much like spelunkers exploring a dangerous cave.

Photos pages 66 & 67: Polly Mullen.

BASEMENT

Getting the shaft: Although the castle contained a historic elevator, a new one had to be carved out to comply with modern-day building codes. Here, Francisco "Pancho" Villa Lobos from Snow Specialty Drilling in Denver, Colo., drills a new 45-foot elevator shaft.

ABOVE – Built to last: The castle rests on a rock-wall foundation.

LEFT– Men at work: Paul Sanchez (left) and Anthony "Bubba" Acosta (right), both with Bradbury Stamm Construction, get down and dirty in the lower depths of the castle.

Photos pages 68 & 69: Polly Mullen.

Photos this page: Polly Mullen.

Remnants of the past: The former mechanical room (top) and billiard room (bottom) were razed to clear space for new accommodations in the basement, such as the student recreation area pictured on the opposite page.

Photo: Chun Y Lai.

Shielded from harm: Fabric protects the walls of the lobby while the room is converted into a workshop during the renovation.

Photos pages 72 & 73: Polly Mullen.

Master craftsman: Anthony "Bubba" Acosta, Bradbury Stamm, applies finishing touches to the castle woodwork.

Before and after: These juxtaposed photographs illustrate the miraculous transformation of the grand staircase in the lobby of the castle.

Photo on left: Polly Mullen. Photo on right: Chun Y Lai.

Shining example: John Latasa of Berkshire Floors Inc. of Albuquerque applies a second coat of varnish to the new maple tongue-and-groove lobby floor.

Photo: Polly Mullen.

Checking in: An ornate reception desk and mailbox anchor the lobby.

Photos pages 76 & 77: Chun Y Lai.

Opulent charm: Spacious and luxuriously equipped, the renovated castle lobby is dedicated to the late King Hussein of Jordan.

Spiraling to new heights: Form meets function
in the graceful lines of this Nautilus staircase.
Photos pages 78 & 79: Polly Mullen.

NAUTILUS STAIRCASE

In deep thought: Asa Haswood of Albuquerque's Bradbury Stamm Construction studies the architectural plans.

Photos pages 80 & 81: Polly Mullen.

STABILIZATION

Solving an architectural challenge: Wooden trusses originally supported the dining room. These could not be reinforced, so pairs of steel trusses were installed to bear the load of the building, while maintaining the open integrity of the spectacular room.

HALLWAYS
◆ ◆ ◆ ◆ ◆ ◆ ◆ ◆ ◆

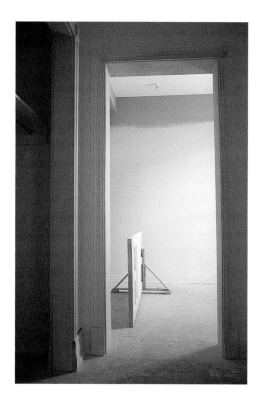

Proceed with great care: The castle hallways threatened to collapse until workers shored up and spruced up the unstable corridors.

Photos pages 82 & 83: Polly Mullen.

Wired: Mike Salas of Bradbury Stamm notches a wall in preparation for laying the building's electrical, phone and computer cables. On the opposite page, an elegant drywall archway punctuates and accentuates the long corridor that follows. Photos pages 84 & 85: Polly Mullen.

Canvassing the construction: Time has damaged these hallowed walls, but hasn't erased the beauty of the colorful rainbow formed by the many exposed layers of old paint.

Photos pages 86 & 87: Polly Mullen.

ROOMS

ABOVE – In the belfry: Tucked away hidden in the attic of the castle are these empty chambers previously used for storage purposes.

OPP0SITE – Simple but sweet: Robert Williams of Preferred Painting, an Albuquerque firm, admires the fruit of his labors

Photos pages 88 & 89: Polly Mullen.

Heavy metal: Radiators (bottom) were replaced by modern centralized heating, while sunlight (top) supplies natural radiance to a vacant room used for storage during the construction process.

Photos pages 90 & 91: Polly Mullen.

Ready for occupancy: Period furniture echoes the classic appeal of this guestroom in the castle.

Victorian splendor: The 1800s castle retains many of its original fixtures, richly suggesting the historic ambience of a bygone era.

Photos pages 92 & 93: Polly Mullen.

DETAILS

  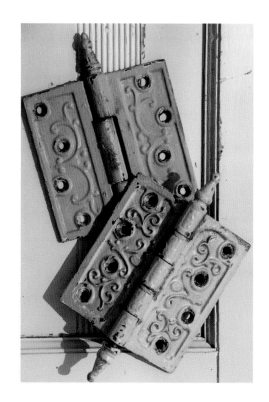

A quick fix: The failure of the original trusses forced workers to install temporary support columns to gird up the magnificent dining room.

Photo: Daniel Martinez.

DINING ROOM

Innovative solutions: Construction crews applied modern science and technical know-how to deal with such formidable puzzles as installing a new elevator, jacking up the sagging ceiling, lifting support beams and overcoming a host of structural challenges. Pictured at work here are Mike Salas and Jesus Morales of Bradbury Stamm (top right), Daniel Leyba of Bradbury Stamm (bottom left) and Larry Franken of Franken Construction and Charles "C.J." Catalano of Bradbury Stamm (bottom right). Photos page 95: Polly Mullen.

Hoisted: A steel channel beam is suspended from the dining room ceiling, awaiting its final placement.

Photos pages 96 & 97: Polly Mullen.

In repose: A silhouetted worker caught amidst the chaos of the dining room construction.

Changing of the guard: Once the province of presidents, nobility and industrial titans, the dining room now accommodates students from around the world.

Photo: Chun Y Lai.

Modern art: Detail from one of the two
hand-blown, Dale Chihuly glass sculptures
that now grace the dining room.
Photo page 99: Polly Mullen.

The United World College's Center for Conflict Resolution as it looked on September 29, 2001, the first public unveiling of the Castle's renovation. Montezuma, NM.

Photo: Polly Mullen

CAMPUS STANDS AS BEACON AGAINST TOWER OF BABEL

BY CRAIG SMITH

Each UWC graduate is potentially a future architect of peace."

– Queen Noor of Jordan

The campus lies secluded in a tree-strewn canyon, the jewel-blue New Mexico sky a high dome above.

Montezuma Castle, that proud relic of former resort days — when celebrities and sightseers came to take the mountain waters and hike the surrounding hills — towers above classrooms, dormitories, offices and playing fields, both guardian and greeter. Everything seems distant, calm, detached.

Appearances can be deceiving. True, the Armand Hammer United World College of the American West in Montezuma, like its nine sister campuses around the globe, is a place where talk is ordered and thought is king.

But calm or quiet? Hardly. Throughout the school year, the place pulses with the life and laughter of hundreds of 16 to 19 year-olds from around the world, there to wrestle with issues of life, self and conflict.

Despite the scores of languages, races and cultures on campus, communication and intent are meant to be crystal clear — a modern refutation of the Tower of Babel.

Here, problems are not feared or shunned: They are the handmaidens of hope.

"We call it the United World College movement for a reason," said UWC-USA President Philip O. Geier. "It's more than an assemblage of campuses. It's intended to create a sense of coherence in the world, to put an overarching concept on global citizenship."

The May 2001 graduation showed that clearly, as 92 students from nearly 60 countries received the coveted International Baccalaureate degree on a sunny New Mexico spring day. For them, it was the culmination of two years of work and reflection — and before that, stiff competition for one of the only 1,000 UWC slots available each year.

Jordan, the United Kingdom, Israel. Norway, South Africa, Bhutan. Hong Kong, Italy, Uganda. Argentina, the United States, Australia. Germany, Ghana, Nepal. Pakistan, Lebanon, Mexico. And many more; the list was an atlas.

These young people were, in a real sense, citizens of the world: custodians of universal potential while still mindful of their countries, faiths and traditions.

"The concept is to help students articulate and represent their own home cultures, but also achieve global citizenship," Geier says. "We now have about 24,000 graduates worldwide committed to that."

ONE WORLD
UNITED

A 1955 Paris meeting of NATO ministers, and leaders active during World War II, sparked the UWC movement. Those leaders sought for ways to lessen Cold War tensions and subsequent hostile feelings.

To assist them, they invited experts of all kinds, from philosophers and activists to spiritual thinkers and practical doers. The goal, said Geier, "was to jump-start their brainstorming."

One of those invited was Kurt Hahn, creator of Outward Bound, that proven combination of experiential learning, emotional growth and team building.

"He laid out his idea of bringing kids together at this most influential age, from 16 to 19," Geier said. "Kurt Hahn believed this was the last best chronological age to really take fresh minds before some degree of cynicism, some degree of pre-professional thought, sets up."

Lord Louis Mountbatten of Burma, another Paris conference participant, established the first campus in 1962 at St. Donat's Castle in Llantwit Major, Wales – Atlantic College. In the years that followed, six more campuses were established.

UWC of Southeast Asia in Singapore; 1971. Lester B. Pearson UWC of the Pacific in Vancouver, Canada, 1974; Waterford Kamhlaba UWC of Southern Africa in Mbabane, Swaziland, 1981; UWC of the Adriatic, Trieste, Italy, 1982; and UWC of the American West in Montezuma, New Mexico, also 1982.

Then came Simón Bolívar UWC of Agriculture in Balinas, Venezuela (1986); Li Po Chun UWC of Hong Kong (1992); Red Cross Nordic UWC in Fjaler, Norway (1995); and Mahindra UWC of India, founded in that country's Maharashtra state in 1997.

While the 10 UWC campuses share the same mission, they are independent in terms of budget and administration. "Think of it as a fleet sailing together, every ship on its own bottom financially," Geier said.

There is an international board, comprised of the chairs of each individual college's governing board. Queen Noor of Jordan is president of the United World Colleges. Nelson Mandela is honorary president of UWC's international council. Queen Elizabeth II is patron of Atlantic College and filmmaker Richard Attenborough of Kamhlaba; explorer Thor Heyerdahl is an international patron.

To be chosen as a UWC student means participation in a veritable mental and emotional Olympics.

"First off, you have highly motivated kids, and they decide they want to be a candidate," Geier said. "It's a competitive process that last year involved kids from 120 countries."

An initial application, with a required essay, begins the process. Applicants' school records are scrutinized, as are scores on standardized tests, as appropriate. Each student must give several personal and educational references, and those persons are closely canvassed.

Those who pass that initial step go on to a personal interview – "How you articulate your values, your youthful but important experience in the world," Geier explained.

As might be expected, the process shrinks the applicant pool considerably.

"In Jordan, for example, we may get perhaps 1,000 applicants a year," Geier pointed out. "That's honed down to 100, then down to 30 to 50. From them, three to four are offered places in one or more campuses." So it goes for all applicants in all countries.

American philanthropist and industrialist Armand Hammer founded the Montezuma campus. Prince Charles, who became involved in UWC through his great-uncle, Lord Mountbatten, introduced Hammer to the movement.

"They had been looking for a U.S. location for a UWC for about a decade," when Hammer became involved, Geier said. Among locations considered were "a deserted Navy island in Boston harbor and a defunct college campus in Vermont."

Why Montezuma, though? A New Mexico town on the southernmost spur of the Sangre de Cristo mountain range; barely a spot on the map; and more than 120 miles away from the nearest international airport. Yet the location was ideal in more ways than one.

Quiet, it would be conducive to study. The wilderness setting was ideal for a combination of academic and experiential learning. For students from other lands, as well as from the rest of the United States, it would mean a new mental and cultural landscape.

And then, there was the Castle.

"Because the parent campus in Wales was built around an old castle, Hammer wanted his college to have some connection with a castle," Geier explained. Montezuma Castle met the bill in name, imposing bulk and availability.

Hammer was UWC-USA's primary supporter until his death in 1990. In the decade since, and under Geier's leadership since 1993, the campus has garnered millions in support from a growing donor roster, enhanced its facilities and completed the Castle's $10 million renovation. The structure thus becomes in reality what it has so long represented: the college's heart.

"Students here are taught to learn how to learn," Geier said. "The curriculum requires them to take six core courses representative of all the traditional liberal arts. They have to take math, natural science, social science, two languages, humanities. So that all of them are well rounded."

Given that, it's fair to say that UWC students are specializing generalists. They choose three of their six subjects to study in depth. The three other subjects receive a less detailed but still comprehensive overview.

There are other courses integral to the concept as well. Theory of Knowledge focuses attention on the nature of knowledge, and encourages exploration of the concept practically and theoretically. A 4,000-word research essay is required. Finally, the "Creativity, Action, Service" program involves each campus family in community service.

It's a reminder that there is more to life than college, and that positive comes via individual efforts.

At Montezuma, students volunteer at the Santa Fe Children's Museum in Santa Fe and take part in more than 30 social service programs in Las Vegas, from Habitat for Humanity to serving as teacher's aides in local public schools. At Mahindra, efforts are devoted to combating poverty and illiteracy. Rural development projects are the touchstone at Simón Bolívar. And so it goes.

The Outward-Bound wilderness-inspired portion of UWC's curriculum varies depending on location. For example, students at Montezuma participate in mountain and backcountry search and rescue teams. At Atlantic College, search and rescue are water- and cliff-based.

Cultural activities are not neglected — music, dance, drama, foodways, customs of different countries and regions, with a focus on the host region. For example, at Red Cross Nordic UWC, it is Nordic studies. At Montezuma, Southwestern studies.

At Montezuma this past year, students also produced Bertolt Brecht's classic of war and its consequences, *Mother Courage and her Children*. An exhibit of student artwork was hung during graduation. Students from Canada and the U.S took part in a "North American Day," with cultural skits covering everything from swing dancing, blues and geography lessons to ebonics and the evening news.

Except at Simón Bolívar, all core UWC instruction is in English. At the Venezuela location, the curriculum is three years; instruction is in Spanish; and a terminal degree in farm administration is available. That college also has a somewhat older student body than the others.

"Bolívar was established at the suggestion of Prince Charles," Geier said. "He felt it was important that we broaden the scope of UWC development, to include the important question of sustainable agriculture, and resources."

The UWC movement has noble aims, but it is eminently practical rather than pie-in-the-sky idealistic. At Montezuma, that means dealing with 200 top achievers who also are still young. Small wonder the student-faculty ratio is 8 to 1.

"We're bringing together the most diverse group of people, but they're also adolescents," Geier pointed out. "They are, in fact, going through all those adjustments that any child does growing up."

In an international setting, that can mean international tensions as well as social or personal ones.

"Last October (2000), when things got heated in the Middle East, we felt very strongly that the students from the Middle East – Israelis, Palestinians, Jordanians, Egyptians –should get together," Geier said. "We huddled with them over a weekend and asked them to make a joint presentation about the problems of the Middle East to the rest of the school."

Another issue arose during the 1999 Serbian conflict.

"There were two Serbian students at the time," Geier said. "I remember them both vividly. One of the two was relatively apolitical and the other was very pro-Western when she came. When the bombing started, both became quite nationalistic.

"One of the women's parents' apartment building was not far from the Chinese Embassy (bombed by NATO). They were quite anxious as kids, as well as (through) their sense of nationality."

Students from surrounding Balkan nations also became drawn into those concerns.

So, "The music teacher sat down with them," Geier recalled. "They found folk songs and other music they had in common. They found a way to produce something jointly while their countries were literally at each other's throats in terms of politics."

UWC goes beyond its campuses to stress that conflict is an inevitable, but potentially positive, force. This is done through "short courses" around the globe, very often in political flashpoint areas.

Their goal is to help young people learn that conflict exists, cannot always be resolved — but need not lead to bloodshed. Past locations have included Jordan, Turkey, Lithuania and Montenegro. Another will take place shortly in Cyprus, bringing together 10 Greek Cypriot and 10 Turkish Cypriot youth.

Conflict resolution also will anchor the castle, via the forthcoming Bartos Institute for the Constructive Engagement of Conflict.

"What can we do to serve the world in a broader way than have 200 16- to 19- year-old residents on campus in New Mexico?" Geier asked. "That, itself, is a pretty major step.

"But we are establishing this institute, and it will be housed in the Castle. We want to help people engage constructively in conflict, rather than thinking we can resolve everything. It will be a place outside the limelight of media, in which real problems can be addressed. And there will be an association of senior fellows involved — leading lights of conflict resolution from around the world."

"So we see the Castle as a venue to not only emphasize what we have traditionally done, but take those new themes to new heights. Montezuma is a physical venue of a series of ideas."

Sitting at the Montezuma graduation, it was impossible not to be impressed with the hope, heart and practical strong-headedness of the United World College movement.

Featured speaker Abiodun Williams encapsulated it superbly. A native of Sierra Leone and a 1979 Pearson College graduate, Williams served with the United Nations' department of peacekeeping operations. He now directs the Ford Foundation's International Fellowships Program.

"UWC students, past and present, have profound experiences in common," Williams said. "We are of every race, nationality and creed, and come from many different lands. Yet, we are bonded together across generations by shared ideals and values . . .

". . . UWC values are as relevant today as ever . . . There can be no viable solutions to our common problems — over-population, famine, refugees, AIDS, environmental degradation and global warming — if nations and peoples do not cooperate and work together for the common good."

For, as Williams pointed out with passion, "Internationalism is not a mere abstraction. It is an imperative. It is the key to the survival of our human race and our fragile planetary home — the Earth."

Montezuma Hotel

Las Vegas Hot Springs, NM

New Mexico Magazine Photo Archives

Photographer unknown

Living in the Long Shadow of the Castle
BY ELMO BACA

Over the years, I have collected memories and memorabilia of the Montezuma. I have lived in its shadow, and I have seen it from afar. I have seen people and life come and go from its hallways and verandas, but have never seen it forsaken completely. The great building with its twin towers makes an indelible impression on all who behold it. Mine is just one remembrance, one *memoria*.

For someone who knows "the Castle" from childhood, exploring its many hidden secrets and moods, the Queen Anne-style hotel no longer conjures an image of architecture so much as one of nostalgia, more of a dramatic stage than a building. The Montezuma Hotel transcended its stone-and-mortar foundations long ago to evolve in my mind as a guardian symbol for the Gallinas high country, for my hometown of Las Vegas and for a vestige of my own youthful innocence.

SKATING THE GALLINAS

The earliest impressions I can summon are those of a grade-school kid during the Kennedy years looking forward each wintry Sunday to ice skating in the canyon. The Montezuma was the majestic beacon to that magical skating pond where the community and the seminarians used to engage in games of tag and crack-the-whip.

Owned by the U.S. Conference of Catholic Bishops at that time, the Montezuma campus was a seminary and home to 100 or 200 (it seemed) young Mexican men training for the priesthood. On weekend afternoons in January and February, long lines of men in black cassocks hugged the sides of the narrow road as our cars ambled by. They would smile and wave at all who passed, their skates tied and looped over their shoulders. The seminarians all had hockey skates; ours were figure.

The skating pond was nestled a mile or so upstream from the hotel. The Atchison, Topeka & Santa Fe Railway had employed nine ponds in Gallinas Canyon as sources of ice for its dining and refrigerator cars. A railroad spur from Las Vegas five miles away ferried the precious cargo of well-to-do tourists and also blocks of ice from the reservoirs.

Sundays at the skating pond were festive and full of frolic. On cold days, a bonfire was built at the base of the awesome, sheer-rock cliff looming over the pond. Next to the parking lot, the "20-30" clubhouse served up hot chocolate. The seminarians were expert skaters, often taking time to give an impromptu lesson or claiming one end of the pond for a walk-on game of hockey.

Rigoberto became our family friend from the skating pond. Two or three years later, he would invite our family to his ordination ceremony held in the old casino building next to the Castle. After the new Catholic priests took their vows, we feasted on roast chicken in the Montezuma's grand dining room. I

MONTEZUMA
MEMORIA

had never seen such a magnificent interior!

After Rigoberto left the Montezuma for his own country, the hotel building receded from my immediate consciousness. Later, when I was approaching my teen-age years in Las Vegas, however, other attractions of Gallinas Canyon appealed to my imagination.

WEALTH IN WATER

Natural, geothermal hot springs clustered down by the Gallinas River below the Castle became accessible to us rambunctious high school students as we acquired driver's licenses. By the time I was attending Robertson High during the Woodstock era, the Mexican priests had left the building, and it was temporarily being "occupied" by a "Chicano power" student group from New Mexico Highlands University.

Montezuma Hotel, Bath House
Las Vegas Hot Springs, NM
From *Harpers Weekly Magazine*
Courtesy of Museum of New Mexico
Neg. No. 170335

For those of us still in high school, however, the allure of the canyon was its soothing hot spring water and the very remote possibility that we could lure girls to enjoy it with us. This romantic notion and the therapeutic qualities of the hot mineral water were among the major compelling reasons that a resort was built in this isolated part of America in the first place. An 1887 promotional brochure on the "Las Vegas Hot Springs" published by the Santa Fe Railroad compares the Montezuma's hot mineral waters favorably to those of Toplitz, Austria and Karlsbad, the Czech Republic.

1846 is a landmark year in Las Vegas history. Not only did Gen. Stephen Watts Kearny and his Army of the West march into the Plaza and ignite the Mexican War, but also Julian and Antonio Donaldson built the first bathhouse in Gallinas Canyon. The Donaldson brothers had astutely petitioned the Las Vegas *alcalde* for a land grant in 1841 – only six years after the tiny village had been founded. Within a decade, the Donaldsons had expanded their modest adobe bathhouse to a larger facility at least 30 feet wide and 100 feet in length and featuring six rooms.

The Donaldsons went bust in 1856, and for a few years thereafter, the property changed hands several times. The Army community at Ft. Union, 20 miles northeast, seems to have been regular patrons of the waters. W. Scott Moore bought the property in 1875, improving its accommodations to an overnight inn. Three weeks after the railroad steamed into Las Vegas on July 4, 1879, a handsome, blue-eyed stranger by the name of Jesse James arrived in Montezuma to take the waters.

DREAMS ARE BUILT AND LOST

With a railroad depot nearby, the fortunes of the hot springs property skyrocketed. Before the sun set on 1879, a Boston corporation called the Las Vegas Hot Springs Company (with major financial support of the A.T. & S.F. railway) had purchased the site and constructed a stone hotel. The "Old Stone Hotel" of 1879-80 offered 14 guestrooms along with a drugstore and a physician's office. The hot springs were cleaned and lined with stone. An advertisement for the Stone Hotel in 1880 boasts shampoos and massages for $1 and a mudpack treatment for $3. The hotel was among the first buildings to be rehabilitated a century later by the Armand Hammer United World College of the American West in 1982.

The Stone Hotel would prove inadequate to meet the Santa Fe Railroad's grandiose plans, along with the public's fascination with resort spas in 1880. By April 1882, a railroad spur had been built to Gallinas Canyon carrying the first passengers to a grand, wooden Montezuma Hotel. The first Montezuma was acclaimed to be the most modern building constructed in the New Mexico Territory up to that time.

Present at the inaugural ball of the Montezuma Hotel on April 17, 1882 was Miguel A. Otero, Jr., future Territorial governor of New Mexico, who later recalled that, "After the banquet the spacious dining hall was cleared of its tables and the floor prepared for the dance. At 9:30, Prof. Hebrin's famous Fourth Cavalry orchestra sounded the grand march and the ball was inaugurated under the most favorable auspices. There were fourteen dances on the program, which kept the 'light fantastic' feet in a bustle till eight in the morning. It was one of the grandest affairs ever given in New Mexico up to that time."

Built to serve 300 guests, the original Montezuma Hotel burned to the ground in a scant few hours in January 1884.

IMAGES REGAINED

A newspaper clipping from the *Las Vegas Daily Optic* of January 17, 1884, mourning "The Montezuma As It Was" surfaced as one of the first items I found in the archives of Highlands University's Donnelly Library in 1978. I was the director of the Photographic Survey of Las Vegas, searching for historic photographs of the community. The news clipping featured an engraving of the enormous Queen Anne-style structure; a building I didn't know had existed. During the next year, I would have the opportunity to examine many more Montezuma photographs, and a fantasy place rich with artistic and literary overtones began to materialize.

The climax of the Photographic Survey project was the publication of dozens of historic photographs in the Centennial edition of the *Las Vegas Daily Optic* on July 27, 1979. The *Optic* sponsored a historic photo contest in recognition of the event, and numerous new images of the community's glorious past emerged. The winning entry in the Montezuma category was a photograph taken about 1885 by the W.E. Hook Wholesale Co. and owned by the late rancher Antonio Sanchez. Mr. Sanchez's winning photo was a panoramic overview of the Montezuma complex, clearly showing the flourishing resort, including spacious bathhouses, railroad depot and landscaped grounds.

The summer of 1979 was thrilling as Las Vegas observed its railroad centennial. A year later, I had the good fortune to meet William ("Wid") Slick, a developer intent on purchasing the Montezuma property. After the Mexican seminarians left for good in 1972, community leaders had unsuccessfully advanced several ideas for the renovation of the hotel, including a Veteran's hospital. Mr. Slick represented the first legitimate development concept for a hotel and conference center in quite a long time.

Nevertheless, the community was stunned in the summer of 1981 to learn that the Montezuma Hotel and its extensive grounds had been purchased by "big California money." Soon, it was revealed that Dr. Armand Hammer, chairman of Occidental Petroleum, had paid a rumored $1 million for the property with the intention of establishing a United World College of the American West. This grand gesture was meant as a tribute to the assassinated Lord Mountbatten, Dr. Hammer's good friend and founder of the United World Colleges (and also the last British Viceroy of India). Undaunted, the Slick family partnered with the Lucero family and other private investors to rehabilitate the Plaza Hotel in Las Vegas in 1982.

True to its fantastic legacy, the Montezuma regained the national spotlight as a prestigious educational institution. Away at graduate school in New York in the spring of 1983, I woke one day to an early morning phone call. "Turn on your TV! Las Vegas is on `The Today Show!'"

Sure enough, there in front of me was the surreal television image of England's Prince Charles being interviewed by "Today Show" anchorwoman Jane Pauley in front of the Montezuma's massive brick fireplace. Prince Charles had led a delegation of royalty and celebrities to the dedication ceremony of the new World College. I could only appreciate the once-in-a-lifetime moment vicariously.

A few years later, about 1986, I would get to witness a landmark event of my own. I was recruited to be a "getaway" friend for one of the first Russian students in residence at the college. My student friend Igor enjoyed trips to Santa Fe to shop at used bookstores. He was amazed by our cheap access to so many books! Later, Igor returned the favor by inviting me to the commencement ceremony in May. It was to be the first graduating class of the United World College, and Dr. Hammer had planned something special.

Beach Boys Surf the Montezuma

Graduation ceremonies began with a luncheon served beneath a great tent pitched on the soccer field. Dr. Hammer addressed the crowd of about 500 people by stating that now that he had fulfilled his goal of establishing the United World College at Montezuma, he could focus his efforts on his next great challenge – finding a cure for cancer. Already in his mid-eighties, Dr. Hammer's energy and dedication inspired everyone.

The afternoon's *pièce de résistance*, however, was to follow. As a gift to the first graduating class, Dr. Hammer had hired the Beach Boys to give a special concert. On one side of the soccer field, with the old powerhouse chimney as a backdrop, engineers had installed a stage flanked by enormous speaker towers. World College students snake-danced to the sappy lyrics of "Be True To Your School" while Dr. Hammer and Hollywood mogul Merv Griffin nodded in approval. In an ironic way, the event recalled the legendary Montezuma ballroom galas of a century before.

A Palimpsest of People and Places

I used to rent a small cottage from John and Emily Gavahan in Montezuma about 1980. A bumpy dirt road twisted beside and behind the "Castle" to the cottage. From my backyard, I could walk down the hill, cross two arroyos and be at Montezuma's rear entrance in five minutes. As it was vacant then, I knew where to find a broken window and sneak in.

I spent several afternoons exploring the labyrinth of the Montezuma. My favorite places were the round rooms of the large tower, where the lack of corners creates spatial illusions and ambiguities. At the top, a ladder and trap door led to the open turret of the soaring tower. From up here, a commanding 360-degree view of Gallinas Canyon and the eastern plains unfolds to infinity.

Look down from the tower through a polarizing filter of time and the penumbra of the original wooden Montezuma appears across the soccer field. My mind's eye can see other ghost structures in the canyon on this clear bright day, but suddenly I am not alone. I am being led on an "official tour" of the monumental rehabilitation of the castle in Spring, 2001. Architects and engineers are explaining on-going repairs to the structure as workmen scurry about like ants below. It's another momentous year in the long saga of the Montezuma, and the hallways will no longer sing their melancholy elegies.

Senator Theater, Baltimore Maryland

Photo: Byrd Wood

These Vintage American Structures Could Crumble For All Time

ENDANGERED LIST

Each year the National Trust for Historic Preservation list of 11 Most Endangered Historic Places identifies important parts of American history that are threatened by neglect, insufficient funds, inappropriate development or insensitive public policy. Since 1988, the 11 Most Endangered list has drawn public attention to more than 120 places.

As in the past 13 years, the choices for 2001 ranged across the country, over time, and through the architectural styles. The most recent year's sites included a modernist icon in New England, a 19th-century Taoist temple in California, and centuries-old buildings along the Río Grande.

While listing does not ensure protection of a site or guarantee funding, the designation has been a powerful tool for raising awareness and rallying resources to save threatened sites in every region of the country.

HISTORIC AMERICAN MOVIE THEATERS, NATIONWIDE

Act One: Since the birth of the motion picture era more than a century ago, millions of Americans have flocked to downtown theaters for the latest films. Historic theaters were designed to transport audiences to fanciful, faraway places with their Art Deco, Egyptian and Chinese motifs, bringing a unique dimension to the moviegoing experience.

Act Two: The multiplex is born. Movie studios gain influence over distribution companies, helping determine which theaters run their films; often, independent, historic theaters are left out of the loop. Many are forced to close, often demolished in the face of staggering competition from suburban multiplexes. Downtowns suffer at the loss of these Main Street anchors.

Bok Kai Temple, Maryville, California
Photo: Friends of Bok Kai

BOK KAI TEMPLE, MARYSVILLE, CALIFORNIA

On the north shore of the Yuba River in the heart of northern California's Sacramento Valley stands a unique testament to the power of tradition — a richly painted Chinese temple. Constructed in 1880 by Chinese immigrants, the Bok Kai Temple long served a flourishing Chinese community first attracted to the area by the California Gold Rush. Boasting exquisite wall paintings and gilded altars, the temple has been the centerpiece of Marysville's Chinese community for more than a century.

Today, though, time and weather have taken their toll, and the temple's murals and furnishings are in jeopardy. In addition, Marysville faces significant economic challenges, and its now dispersed Chinese community lacks the resources to face the daunting task of restoring the temple and its collection alone.

Valley floor, present
Photo: Doug Beery

TELLURIDE VALLEY FLOOR, TELLURIDE, COLORADO

No one disputes that Telluride is one of the Rocky Mountains' most beloved vacation spots. The problem is, it's being loved to death.

Nestled among 14,000-foot peaks, Telluride is cradled in a wide valley that, until now, remained as verdant and peaceful as when the Ute Indians hunted there centuries ago. But sprawl has come to the mountains, and now a massive resort may be developed on the 880-acre valley floor, threatening the region's historic context and forever altering one of the Rocky Mountains' last intact mining towns.

Wilde Building
Photo: Campaign to Save Connecticut General

CIGNA CAMPUS, BLOOMFIELD, CONNECTICUT

A widely publicized architectural icon that was once hailed as one of "ten buildings in America's future" could soon be a thing of the past.

When it was completed in 1957, the headquarters of the Connecticut General Life Insurance Company in Bloomfield, Conn., was immediately recognized as a milestone in the history of modern architecture. Five years later, similar praise was heaped on the headquarters of the Emhart Corporation, built just a short distance away. Now CIGNA Corporation, the owner of both buildings, wants to demolish them and turn the beautifully landscaped site into a sprawling complex of offices, stores and houses clustered around a golf course.

CARTER G. WOODSON HOUSE, WASHINGTON, D.C.

Eighty-five years after Carter G. Woodson created the black history movement, the Washington home where he lived and worked sits abandoned and forgotten, an ironic legacy of the man who spent his life preserving African-American history and culture.

The Victorian 1890s red brick rowhouse with the broken windows and overgrown yard sits squarely in the middle of D.C.'s Shaw neighborhood, a richly historic area undergoing a renaissance. While many of Shaw's grand old homes and classic row houses have been rehabbed, the Woodson home, whose condition worsens by the day, awaits rescue.

Exterior
Photo: ASALH

FORD ISLAND, PEARL HARBOR, HONOLULU, HAWAII

The historic resources remaining from one of the most painfully memorable events in American military history – the attack on Pearl Harbor – are in danger of being lost through a massive development initiative at Pearl Harbor's Ford Island in Honolulu.

The December 7, 1941, attack on Pearl Harbor is seared into the memory of Americans to this day. Ford Island – the centerpiece of the Pearl Harbor National Historic Landmark District – is adjacent to Battleship Row, now home to the USS Missouri Memorial Association, and a few yards away from the memorial to the USS Arizona, which sustained the heaviest loss of life that day. Remnants of bomb craters and signs of the Japanese aircraft's strafing runs are still visible. The original airfield, air tower, World War II hangars, a collection of bungalows, officers' housing and landscaping with mature Banyan trees remain on the site. Yet these historic resources could be altered forever if there is inadequate planning to protect them.

Air tower
Photo: David Scott

MILLER-PURDUE BARN, GRANT COUNTY, INDIANA

They are simple feasts for the unhurried, appreciative eye. Historic barns – whether rugged stone or red-painted wood – add life and color to the rural landscape. In northeast Indiana, an English-style, pre-Civil War barn faithfully served the Miller farm for nearly a century.

But as the farming economy changes, old barns like the Millers' are increasingly viewed as obsolete, and across the country, many owners are choosing to dispose of historic barns – either by torching them or neglecting them – rather than consider adapting them for modern farming or other uses.

Exterior
Photo: Wayne Townsend

Exterior, Farm
Photo: Preservation Association of Lincoln

STEVENS CREEK SETTLEMENTS, LINCOLN, NEBRASKA

Days and nights are generally quiet along Stevens Creek, where the rural landscape rings with the music of birds and the buzz of crickets. But if current plans are carried out, these bucolic sounds could be drowned out by the rumble of bulldozers and the roar of traffic – and a long-cherished way of life could disappear forever.

Set in a gently rolling landscape just east of Lincoln, the fertile Stevens Creek valley has been considered prime agricultural land for more than a century, and many of its farms are still owned by descendants of the first settlers. Those farmers - plus the bikers and hikers who treasure the area's quiet beauty – now face the threat of a proposed expressway and associated development that will bring noise, traffic and sprawl to this region of fields, woods and history.

Abandoned Church near Luverne, North Dakota
Photo: Jim Lindberg

PRAIRIE CHURCHES OF NORTH DAKOTA

Were it not for the prairie church, the vast North Dakota landscape would stretch unbroken to the horizon. Often founded by first-generation settlers from Germany, Poland, Iceland, Russia and Scandinavia, the simple prairie church was usually the first building to go up when a town was settled - and the last to close its doors if the community died out.

But now many of these buildings are threatened. Of North Dakota's 2,000 church structures, more than 400 are vacant and threatened by inadequate maintenance and demolition.

Jesus Treviño Fort, San Ygnacio, Texas
Photo: Mario Sánchez

LOS CAMINOS DEL RÍO, LOWER RÍO GRANDE VALLEY, TEXAS

For much of its history, the sun-baked Lower Río Grande Valley of Texas has been a place where time moves slowly. But now the future is rushing in at breakneck speed, and much of the region's heritage is in danger of being swept away.

Stretching for 200 miles between the cities of Laredo and Brownsville, the area known as "Los Caminos del Río" encompasses farms and ranches, fast-growing cities and dusty small towns whose history and architecture reflect a rich blend of Hispanic, Latino and Anglo cultures. The region is also a patchwork of newfound economic prosperity and longstanding poverty – a perplexing paradox that has thwarted efforts by agencies on both sides of the US-Mexican border to preserve historic buildings and neighborhoods, and encourage heritage tourism.

Jackson Ward Historic District, Richmond, Virginia

There's a reason why the Jackson Ward Historic District is called the "Harlem of the South." Since the late 19th century, this neighborhood in Richmond, Va., has been one of America's largest African-American districts, once bursting with the sounds of jazz and prosperity.

But in the 1950s, highway construction ripped Jackson Ward in two, an act that started decades of urban decline. And now Jackson Ward is in danger of losing its heritage forever.

100 block, East Clay
Photo: Historic Jackson Ward Association, Inc.

If you're interested in learning more about places on the National Trust for Historic Preservation's Most Endangered list, or you'd like to support the Trust's efforts to protect our irreplaceable heritage, you can become a member on-line at http://www.nthp.org. Included in your membership is a subscription to the award-winning *Preservation* magazine and reduced or free admission to the Trust' 20 historic sites.

If you'd like to nominate a site for next 11 Most Endangered list, you can download a nomination form from the Web site.

You can also e-mail the Trust or call toll-free at 1-800-315-NTHP.

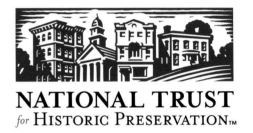

NATIONAL TRUST *for* **HISTORIC PRESERVATION**™

New Mexico Heritage Preservation Alliance

What are the most significant historic places in New Mexico currently in need of prompt attention or else they risk fading into the sunset? Here are the top 10 candidates for a little tender, loving care, according to the New Mexico Heritage Preservation Alliance. Visit the non-profit organization's Web site at http://www.nmheritage.org or call (505) 989-7745 to find out how you can help or to nominate historic places for future consideration by the group. Eligible resources must be 50 years or older, within the boundaries of New Mexico, and significant from either a cultural or architectural standpoint or both. The nominees, though, can encompass all manner of buildings, houses and structures, as well as broader sites and historic districts, ruins and cultural landscapes.

"The Alliance has seen how effective endangered designation can be in changing the disposition of a threatened resource and looks forward to working with communities across the state to save this year's list," said Katherine "Kak" Slick, president of the New Mexico Heritage Preservation Alliance.

The 2001 Endangered List:

Buffalo Mountain (Santa Fe County):

Significance: This double-ridged hill strongly resembles a buffalo and is part of the cultural landscape of the Cerrillos Hills. Native American shrines and links to Spanish and Anglo mining, ranching and commerce give the area an identity, define its character and constitute its heritage.

Threat: A proposed mining operation will remove millions of tons of gravel annually and destroy the body of the "buffalo," leaving a pit in its place.

Cavate Pueblos (Los Alamos County):

Significance: The Cavate Pueblos are found throughout the Pajarito Plateau, with concentrations in Frijoles Canyon and Tsankawi at Bandelier National Monument. The pueblos are groups of rooms carved into the volcanic tuff cliffs. They are the ancestral homes to the Tewa and Keres people, whose descendants still reside in the area. The *cavates* are unusual in the Prehistoric Pueblo record, and possess fragile features seldom found in archaeological sites.

Threat: The *Cavate* Pueblos are threatened by erosion and weathering. Geologically, the Bandelier tuff from which the cavates are carved is variably welded, soft and porous. The tuff is inherently weak.

DEMING TRAIN DEPOT (THE TOWN OF DEMING):

Significance: The Deming Train Depot has been an integral part of the history of Deming. It has been visited by five presidents as well as the Liberty Bell on tour. In 1881, it was the site of the completion of the Southern Transcontinental rail connection designated with a silver spike. It was also a Harvey House from 1881 to 1930.

Threat: There are concerns about the future status of the building, including worries about its demolition. Southern Pacific employees vacated the building two years ago due to disrepair. Little work has been done to correct the deterioration.

FIRST NATIONAL BANK BUILDING OF EDDY COUNTY (THE TOWN OF CARLSBAD):

Significance: This building is one of the first permanent buildings in the area. Constructed of local brick in 1890 with a mail-order iron façade, it was part of the Pecos Valley Land and Development Company's efforts to assure potential land buyers that their irrigation scheme was not a fly-by-night operation. The building was placed on the National Register of Historic Places in 1965.

Threat: Long-term neglect is the chief threat to this property. The original masonry work is soft and crumbling, the iron façade is rusting and the woodwork is deteriorating. The foundation, second-floor supports and electrical system are in serious disrepair.

HISTORIC COMMERCIAL SIGNS ON ROUTE 66 (STATEWIDE):

Significance: The commercial roadside signs have been a primary means of communicating to the public since the beginning of the Age of the Automobile. Many of these signs are important for their cues to a place's identity – the Uranium Cafe in Grants, for example. Tourists consider the historic signs to be an intrinsic part of the Route 66 experience.

Threat: New construction, redevelopment and urban sprawl destroy these historic signs. In Albuquerque alone, nearly half the signs listed on a map from 1987 are no longer in place and many of the neon signs are no longer operational.

Photo: Mike Pitel

NEW MEXICO'S NEW DEAL PUBLIC ART (STATEWIDE):

Significance: The New Deal during the Great Depression funded numerous artists in New Mexico. They produced 65 murals and large paintings, 650 smaller paintings, 10 sculptures, and numerous other items including photographs, furniture, *retablos*, *santos*, and pottery. The art of the New Deal recorded the way that New Mexicans worked, lived and played during the 1930s and 1940s.

Threat: The public art of the New Deal is showing its age. It needs to be maintained and conserved so that future generations can appreciate the art. Some of the collections are neglected and stored in places unsuitable for preserving delicate paintings. And some of the art has been lost or stolen.

OSCAR HUBER MEMORIAL GRANDSTAND AND BALLPARK (THE TOWN OF MADRID, SANTA FE COUNTY):

Significance: The grandstand and ballpark were the focus of the community in the old coal mining days. The ballpark was the first in the state to have lights for night games. It also has held rodeos, horse races, and a toy village with a miniature train for children as part of the famous Madrid Christmas Celebration.

Threats: The grandstand is endangered due to normal structural disintegration, mostly from the period when Madrid was a ghost town. As an old stone and wood structure, it needs maintenance and preservation to restore its original look.

RED BRICK SCHOOL BUILDING (THE TOWN OF TULAROSA, OTERO COUNTY):

Significance: The Red Brick School provided the opportunity for a better life through education at a time when few children had the opportunity to attend school. Completed in 1917, the Red Brick School Building is part of the Tularosa Original Townsite District, which is on the National Register of Historic Places, and the New Mexico Register of Cultural Resources. Furthermore, the building was designed by Trost and Trost, significant Southwestern architects.

Threat: The Red Brick School Building has been unoccupied since the early 1970s and neglect has been its worst enemy. In addition to gradual physical decline, there is a large hole in the roof, pigeons have fouled the interior, and windows are broken and boarded up.

RÍO GRANDE THEATER (THE CITY OF LAS CRUCES):

Significance: Built in 1926, the Río Grande Theater was an important part of Las Cruces' downtown business district. It served as a meeting place for people until 1998 when it closed its doors.

Threat: As a two-story adobe building, the Río Grande Theater is structurally vulnerable. Its exposed adobes, broken windows, and fractured front of the building need to be stabilized. The current owner, the Doña Ana Arts Council, needs to raise $1,000,000 to fully renovate the exterior of the building to its original condition and the interior to a state-of-the-art performance center.

TRUBY'S TOWER AND THREE CORN RUINS (SAN JUAN COUNTY):

Significance: Truby's Tower and Three Corn Ruins represent classic examples of Navajo pueblito architecture dating to the 18th century. These sites are not only significant for their standing architecture, but their potential to contribute to archaeological studies. Furthermore, the sites are within the area identified as Dinetah, the Navajo Ancestral homeland.

Threat: Natural erosive forces as well as human impacts are contributing to the deterioration of Truby's Tower and Three Corn Ruins. The general condition of the architecture, exposure of the masonry, vandalism and other factors leave these in danger of catastrophic structural failure.

NEW MEXICO HERITAGE PRESERVATION ALLIANCE MISSION STATEMENT

The New Mexico Heritage Preservation Alliance is a statewide, private organization dedicated to the protection, preservation and stewardship of New Mexico's cultural properties. These properties include buildings, districts and sites of historical, architectural and archaeological significance, and the cultural landscape.

The purpose of the New Mexico Heritage Preservation Alliance is to promote an awareness of and respect for all that is culturally significant and distinctive about New Mexico and, through these efforts, to keep alive and intact for the enrichment of present and future generations the unique multicultural heritage of New Mexico.

ABOUT THE CONTRIBUTORS

ELMO BACA serves as director of the New Mexico State Historic Preservation Division. A native of Las Vegas, New Mexico, he helped found the Citizen's Committee for Historic Preservation in that city and was a general manager for La Plaza Vieja Partneship, Inc., which rehabilitated 15 buildings in Las Vegas during the 1980s. He is a former director of the New Mexico Main Street Program and author of many books, including *Romance of the Mission, Native American Style: Harmonious and Spiritual Interiors* and *Santa Fe Fantasy: The Quest for the Golden City.*

JON BOWMAN is associate publisher of *New Mexico Magazine* and executive director of the Santa Fe Film Festival. A movie critic for nearly 30 years, he is the author or co-author of six books, one screenplay and countless magazine and newspaper articles appearing in the *Hollywood Reporter, Friendly Exchange* and the Japanese edition of *Esquire*, among other periodicals.

DR. PHILIP O. GEIER, a historian, has served for the past eight years as president of the United World College, whose campus includes the Montezuma Castle. Over his 25-year career in international education, he has taught at Syracuse University, Dickinson College and the Sorbonne in Paris. He has held leadership positions with the French-American Foundation, the American Farm School in Greece, World Learning and the Fulbright Association in Washington, D.C., and is a member of the Council on Foreign Relations in New York and the Pacific Council on International Policy in Los Angeles.

NANCY HANKS worked at the New Mexico State Historic Preservation Division from 1998 to 2001 as database manager and architectural historian. She currently is with the City of Chicago Landmarks Division, where she prepares landmark nominations. She holds a doctorate degree in historical geography from the University of Oklahoma.

POLLY MULLEN, artist, designer, photographer, desires to make a positive difference. She lives in Montezuma and has worked for the past several years as a free-lance photographer for the Armand Hammer United World College of the American West. She is a commercial as well as a fine-art black-and-white photographer, whose images have graced the pages of *New Mexico Magazine*, *Rocky Mountain Magazine*, *The Santa Fean*, and *Arts and Antiques Magazine*.

CRAIG A. SMITH is classical music critic of *The Santa Fe New Mexican* and a staff writer for its weekly arts magazine "Pasatiempo". He produced and edited a special *Santa Fe New Mexican* magazine supplement on the renovation of Santa Fe's historic Lensic Theater and co-edited the paper's landmark 150th anniversary history in 1999. His research interests include opera, British political history and the social history of food.

MARK THALER, project architect for the Montezuma Castle restoration, works for Einhorn Yaffee Prescott Architecture & Engineering, PC of Albany, New York. The firm is a leader in the historic preservation sphere, credited with helping preserve or renovate such landmark sites as the Lincoln Memorial and Jefferson Memorial, Ellis Island National Historic Site, Arlington National Cemetery, the Edgar Allan Poe House in Philadelphia and the U.S. Military Academy at West Point.

HEIDI UTZ has served as an editor for *Outside Magazine*, *Mothering Magazine*, and John Muir Publications, and has also published features in *New Mexico Magazine* and *E: The Environmental Magazine*. Based in Santa Fe for the past decade, she specializes in the arts, especially film and music. Heidi has also completed three children's books and is currently writing a volume of essays. She has been in involved in historic preservation efforts and has used her carpentry skills to build homes for Habitat for Humanity, both in New Jersey and New Mexico.

SUGGESTED READINGS

◆　　◆　　◆　　◆　　◆　　◆

Want to find out more about the Montezuma Castle, the United World College or the colorful history of Las Vegas, New Mexico? Here are a few valuable sources to whet your appetite.

BOOKS

America's Grand Resort Hotels, by Jeffrey Limerick, Nancy Ferguson, Richard Oliver. New York: Pantheon Books, 1979.

The Architecture of John Wellborn Root, by Donald N. Hoffman. Baltimore: Johns Hopkins University Press, 1973.

A Brief History of New Mexico, by Myra Ellen Jenkins and Albert H. Schroeder. Albuquerque: University of New Mexico Press, 1974.

Dreams and Promises: The Story of the Armand Hammer United World College: A Critical Analysis, by Theodore D. Lockwood, Santa Fe: Sunstone Press, 1997.

Gateway to Glorieta: A History of Las Vegas, New Mexico, by Lynn I. Perrigo. Boulder: Pruett Publishing, 1982.

Las Vegas, New Mexico: A Portrait, photographs by Alex Traube, text by E.A. Mares, Albuquerque: University of New Mexico Press, 1983.

Seven Trails West, by Albert King Peters. New York: Abbeville Press, 1996.

Virgin Land: The American West as Symbol and Myth, by Henry Nash Smith, Cambridge: Harvard University Press, 1950.

Wildest of the Wild West: True Tales of a Frontier Town on the Santa Fe Trail, by Howard Bryan, Santa Fe: Clear Light Publications, 1991.

Windows on the Past: Historic Lodging of New Mexico, by Sandra Lynn. Albuquerque: University of New Mexico Press, 1999.

MAGAZINE, NEWSPAPER ARTICLES

"A Campus Where the World Meets," by Rosemary Zibart, *Christian Science Monitor*, November 28, 2000.

"Castle of Their Dreams," by Zelie Pollon, *Dallas Morning News*, November 6, 2000.

"Crumbling Montezuma Castle On Most Endangered List," by Monica Soto, *The Santa Fe New Mexican*, June 17, 1997.

Las Vegas Daily Optic. A goldmine of original source material with articles on Montezuma dating back to the 1870s.

"The Las Vegas Hot Springs," by Clarence Pullen, *Harper's Weekly*, June 28, 1890.

"The Montezuma Hotel," by Louise Harris Ivers, in *New Mexico Architecture*, May-June 1977.

"New Mexico Castle Is Again On the Rise," by Dennis W. Roberts, *Southwest Contractor*, February 1, 2001.

"Steel Revives Historic Structure," by Marie Ennis, P.E., Einhorn Yaffee Prescott, *Modern Steel Construction*, January 2001.

"United World College: An International Challenge in Education," by April Kopp, *New Mexico Magazine*, June 1985.

INDEX

◆ ◆ ◆ ◆ ◆ ◆

Adobe Hotel *10, 12, 21*

Americans with Disabilities Act 36

Andrews & Co., fireplace designers, 15

Atchison, Topeka & Santa Fe Railway 6, 11-12,
        15-16, 19, 22-24, 28-29, 31, 107-110

Attenborough, Richard 102

Bandelier National Monument 118

Bartos Institute for the Constructive Engagement
        of Conflict 5-6, 21, 39, 105

Barney, Capt. J.W. 24

Bath house, *17, 22, 23, 108*

Beach Boys 111

Billy the Kid 12, 21

Bok Kai Temple 114

Bollinger, Barney 24

Bradbury Stamm Construction 33, *64, 69, 73, 80,
        84, 95*

Brecht, Bertolt 104

Brewster, Mr. and Mrs. J.W. 24

Buffalo Mountain 118

Burro trips 23

Burnham and Root, architects 15-16, 29

Callen, Milton W. 22

Carter G. Woodson House 115

Casino 19, 23, 31, 107

Cavate Pueblos 118

Charles L. Page & Co., furniture designers 15

Chihuly, Dale 36, *99*

Chinese immigrants 114

Citizens' Committee for Historic Preservation 4,
        7, 17-18, 32, 35, 37-38

CIGNA Campus 114

Collins, Judy 25

Davis, Shelby M.C. 6, 25

Deming Train Depot 119

Doña Ana Arts Council 121

Donaldson, Julian and Antonio 12, 108

Duke of Rutland 24

Einhorn Yaffee Prescott Architecture &
        Engineering, PC 33, 123, 125

Ferrell, Catherine 39

First National Bank Building of Eddy County 119

Flynn, Jim 25

Forbes, Malcolm 25

Ford Island, Pearl Harbor 115

Ford, Robert 21

Fort Union 12

Franken Construction Company 33, *61*

Fremont, John 24

Gallinas Canyon 12, 28-29, 107-109, 111

Gallinas River 15, 108

Gavahan, John and Emily 111

Gilded Age 27

Glass, Philip 25

Gothic Revival architecture 30

Governor's Committee on Concerns of the
        Handicapped 34

Grand Canyon 19, 25, 31

Grant, Ulysses S. 23, 31

Griffin, Merv 111

Hahn, Kurt 102

Hammer, Armand 5, 25, 101, 109-111

Harper's Weekly, magazine 12, 23, 125

Harvey, Fred 31, 119

Hayes, Rutherford B. 24

Heyerdahl, Thor 102

Hot springs 10, 12-16, 21-23, 26, 28, 30, 106,
        108-109, 125

Hunting 24

Jackson Ward Historic District 117

James, Jesse 12, 21-22, 31, 109

Jerome, Rice, Moore and Emory, architects 12

Johnson, Gov. Gary 25

Karlsbad, The Czech Republic 22-23, 108

Kearny, Gen. Steven Watts 108

King Hussein 34, 77

Landers, Ann 25

Las Vegas Hot Springs Company 12, 109

Las Vegas Hot Springs Hotel 12, 21-22

Hot Springs Hotel

Las Vegas Optic, newspaper 22, 24-25, 28, 41,
        109-110, 125

Los Caminos del Río 116

Mandela, Nelson 102

Manners, Lady Diana 24

Marquis of Lorne 24

Mexican War 108

Miller-Purdue Barn 115

Montezuma, Aztec ruler 21

Montezuma Baptist College 25

Montezuma closing 19, 25

Montezuma Courier, newspaper 24

Montezuma, first fire, 1884, 15, 22, 109

Montezuma, second fire, 1885, 16, *18*, 31

Montezuma Hotel *14*, 17, 22, 26-27, 30, 32, 35,
        37-38, 41, 106-110, 125
    Aviary 22
    Basement 23, 34, 36-37, *66-71*
    Bay windows 15
    Billiard parlor 23, 34, *70*
    Bowling alley 31, 24, *66*
    Chandeliers 31, 36
    Dining room 12, 16, 23, 31-*32*, 34, 36, *81,
        94, 99*
    Doors *64-65*
    Dormers 15, 29
    Electricity 16, 36
    Fireplace 15, 23, 30, *38-39*, 41, 110

Furnishings 23, 30, *35*, 114

Gables 15, 29

Gardens 23, 27-28

Hallways *82-85*

Kitchen 28, 31, 34, 36

Lobby 15-16, 23-24, *30*, 34, 38-39, *72-77*

Nautilus staircase *78-79*

Parlors 12, 16, 23, 30, *35*

Roof 15, 29, 31, 34, 37-38, *58-59* 120

Rooms *86-91*

Sewing rooms 23

Stained glass windows 15, 29-30, 36, 39

Towers 15, 29-30, 36, 38, *50-51, 56*, 101, 107, 111

Trusses 34, 36, *81*

Turret *47*

Verandas 12, 15, 28-29, *30*, 37-39, *48-49, 54-55, 57*, 107

Windows *60-63*

Wine cellar 22

Zoo 31

Montezuma Ideals 22

Montezuma Seminary 5, 39, 107

Moore, Harriet 29

Moore, W. Scott 21, 109

Mountbatten, Lord Louis 41, 102-103, 110

Movie theaters 113

National Trust for Historic Preservation 5, 33, 113, 117

Neal Deal Public Art 120

New Mexico Heritage Preservation Alliance 118, 121

New Mexico Highlands University 108-109

New Mexico State Historic Preservation Division 34, 122-123

North Dakota Prairie Churches 116

Oddfellows Lodge 24

Old Stone Hotel 4, 12, 109

Ollila, Jorma 25

Oscar Huber Memorial Grandstand and Ballpark 120

Otero, Miguel A. Jr., New Mexico Territorial governor 109, 120

Outward Bound 102

Panic of 1893, 19

Pauley, Jane 41, 110

Payette, Julie 25

Phoenix Hotel 16, 21, 31

Photographic Survey of Las Vegas 109

Plaza Hotel 41, 110

Price, George W. 24

Prince Charles 5, 25, 41, 103-104, 110

Princess Louise 24

Queen Anne architecture 15, 28-31

Queen Elizabeth II, 102

Queen Noor *8, 9*, 25, 101-102

Queen Victoria 24

Red Brick School, Tularosa 120

Reservoir Hill 15, 29

Richardson, Bill 5-6, 25

Río Grande Theater 121

Roosevelt, Teddy *20*, 23, 31

Route 66 Historic Signs 119

Sanchez, Antonio 110

Sangre de Cristo Mountains 12, 23, 28, 103

Santa Fe Trail 11, 124

Sherman, Gen. William Tecumseh 24

Slick, Katherine "Kak" 5, 118

Slick, William 110

Speare, Alden 12

Stevens Creek Settlements 116

Street, George W. 22-23

Tamme Opera House 24

Telluride Valley 114

Three Corn Ruins 121

Toplitz, Austria 108

Trost and Trost, architects 120

Truby's Tower 121

Turner, Frederick Jackson 11-12, 19

United Nations 6, 25, 105

United World College 5-6, 9, 25, 33, 41, 101, 105, 109-110, 122-125

United World College campuses

   Adriatic campus, Trieste, Italy 102

   Armand Hammer UWC of the American West, Montezuma, U.S.A. 6, 11, 41, 101-102, 109-110, 123-124

   Atlantic college, Llantwit Major, Wales 102

   Lester B. Pearson campus, Vancouver, Canada 102

   Li Po Chun UWC, Hong Kong 102

   Mahindra UWC, India 102, 104

   Red Cross Nordic UWC, Fjaler, Norway 102, 104

   Simón Bolívar UWC of Agriculture, Balinas, Venezuela 102, 104

   UWC of Southeast Asia, Singapore 102

   Waterford Kamhlaba campus, Mbabane, Swaziland, 102

United World College curriculum, 102-104

U.S. Conference of Catholic Bishops 107

W.E. Hook Wholesale Company 110

White House Millennium Council 5, 33

Williams, Abiodun 25, 105

Wingert, Laban 33

Yellowstone 27